RICHARD BRINSLEY
SHERIDAN

THE RIVALS
and
THE SCHOOL FOR
SCANDAL

ILLUSTRATED BY
RENÉ BEN SUSSAN

~~~ *MRS. MALAPROP* ~~~

THE RIVALS
and
THE SCHOOL
FOR SCANDAL

TWO COMEDIES BY
RICHARD BRINSLEY SHERIDAN

WITH INTRODUCTORY NOTES BY
JOHN MASON BROWN
AND
CARL VAN DOREN
AND ILLUSTRATIONS BY
RENÉ BEN SUSSAN

LONDON

PRINTED AT THE CURWEN PRESS
FOR THE HERITAGE PRESS OF NEW YORK

PRINTED IN GREAT BRITAIN

THE RIVALS : A COMEDY

AS PERFORMED
AT THE THEATRES ROYAL
IN DRURY LANE
AND COVENT GARDEN

CONTENTS

A LIST OF THE PLATES

INTRODUCTION

'SHERRY is dull, naturally dull; but it must have taken him a great deal of pains to become what we now see him. Such an excess of stupidity, Sir, is not in Nature.' With these splenetic words Dr. Johnson once dispatched old Tom Sheridan, lecturer, writer, and actor, and father of Richard Brinsley Sheridan.

No one, however crabbed his mood, could have described Tom's son in such terms. The brilliance of the author of *The Rivals* was of a kind that invited hyperbole. Of all the eulogies heaped upon him none is more famous than Lord Byron's, 'Whatever Sheridan has done or chosen to do, has been, *par excellence*, always the best of its kind. He has written the best comedy, *The School for Scandal*; the best opera, *The Duenna*—in my mind far before that St. Giles' lampoon, the *Beggar's Opera*; the best farce, *The Critic*—it is only too good for an afterpiece; and the best address, *The Monologue on Garrick*; and to crown all, delivered the very best oration, the famous Begum speech, ever conceived or heard in this country.'

Byron, when he released his superlatives, was thinking of the Sheridan whose public performances had amazed his contemporaries by their genius and versatility. Sheridan's private life was decidedly less dazzling. It was a success story (really two success stories, considering his triumphs in two careers) which had an unhappy ending. After a glittering beginning it became grubby. A. B. Walkley years ago summarized it in these tart terms, 'The scapegrace son of an eccentric father and grandson of a *grandpère prodigue*, Sheridan eloped with a public singer, wrote three good plays, mismanaged a great theatre, made a couple of great parliamentary speeches, drank a great deal too much claret and brandy, treated two good wives uncommonly ill, put his trust in a prince, was ruined, and died a broken, starving man'. When it comes to Sheridan's having treated the beautiful Elizabeth Ann Linley 'uncommonly ill', Walkley

7

wrote contrary to the evidence of the many who have insisted that, in spite of his volatile disposition, Sheridan was a devoted husband. Elsewhere Walkley's summary is as accurate as it is stark.

Just before he died and right after his death, the great world in which Sheridan had moved renewed its recognition of him for a moment. Unfortunately, this moment came as no more than an empty epilogue to a play that had gone to pieces in its last act. The titled friends, who for some time had forgotten him and allowed his creditors to close in, suddenly remembered Sheridan —too late. The public, which had doted on him in his golden years, developed a new but belated affection for him when it learned how shabbily he had been treated in his poverty and illness. There was an elaborate funeral with earls and lords and even two royal dukes present. As a final honor, he was buried in the Poets' Corner of Westminster Abbey.

That Sheridan merited a place in the Abbey is beyond denial. Whether he himself would have chosen the Poets' Corner is questionable. When he died in his sixty-fifth year on 7 July 1816, his playwriting days (except for *Pizarro*, the dreary adaptation he made from Kotzebue just before the century's turn) were far behind him. To be sure, he had been the manager, rather the mismanager, of Drury Lane from 1776 until 1809 when, on a night fatal to his fortunes, the theatre burned. But the center of his interest had long since been transferred from make-believe to the drama of reality. He had been an outstanding member of the House of Commons for thirty-two years (1780–1812), a dramatist for only four (1775–9).

No orator in an age of great orators was more admired. He spoke frequently on many issues, most of them now forgotten, and again and again showed how uncommon was his eloquence, how effective his wit. He was the private friend and public champion of the Prince Regent. In the first days of the French Revolution he argued with brilliance against English interference. With the same brilliance he opposed the methods being used to abolish the Irish Parliament, and warned Britain of the dangers presented to her by Napoleon. His greatest triumphs as a speaker, however, were achieved during the trial of Warren Hastings.

The passage in which Macaulay sets the stage for those proceedings is one of the most colorful evocations of a dramatic event known to English prose. Yet, even before Sheridan spoke with spectacular success at the trial, he had made in the House the Begum speech referred to by Byron. The impression it produced, says Macaulay, 'was such as has never been equaled. He sat down, not merely amidst cheering, but amidst the loud clapping of hands, in which the Lords below the bar and the strangers in the gallery joined. The excitement of the House was such that no other speaker could obtain a hearing; and the debate was adjourned. . . . Within four and twenty hours, Sheridan was offered a thousand pounds for the copyright of the speech, if he would himself correct it for the press.' By common consent at the time, and even twenty years later as remembered by so masterful an orator as Fox, Sheridan's Begum speech was the best ever made in the House of Commons.

Because of such triumphs on such a scene Sheridan might have preferred (had he had any choice in the matter) to rest in the Abbey in the company of Fox and Pitt, with whom he had played a major part in the pageant of empire, instead of being placed close to Garrick among the artists and writers. But he would have been wrong. He would have succumbed to the common Philistine fallacy that the man of action is more important than the man of letters. He would have overestimated the abiding qualities of his contributions to politics and underestimated the lasting merits of his comedies. The importance of the real problems he argued in Parliament would have tempted him into believing that his plays were unimportant because their major concern was delight.

The irony of Sheridan's fate is, of course, that the ringing words he spoke in the House are dimly remembered, whereas the best of the comedies he wrote for his playhouse have continued over the years to be very much alive. *St. Patrick's Day* may now be an almost forgotten farce. *The Duenna*, in spite of Byron's praise of it and the high esteem in which it was once held, may be an operetta which is rarely played. *A Trip to Scarborough* may have few admirers. Even *The Critic*, notwithstanding its uproarious moments, may be a parody of somewhat special interest. But *The Rivals* and *The School for Scandal* are known the world over, and because of them so is Sheridan.

The two comedies are quite different in tone, quality, and approach. Hard as it is to believe, *The Rivals* was written in 1774 when Sheridan was twenty-three, *The School for Scandal* three years later when he had achieved the ripe old age of twenty-six. In Sheridan's case it is necessary to insist that twenty-six was really a venerable age because he had by then matured so incredibly as a comic dramatist.

Everyone knows that England's best comedies are written by Irishmen. At least from Congreve and Farquhar down to Wilde and Shaw, most of the beacon-lights of English comedy have been men born or educated in John Bull's other island. Sheridan was no exception. Neither was Goldsmith with whom, rightly or wrongly, he is often linked. The two of them at about the same time dispelled the darkness which had fallen on comic writing in England since Congreve dwindled into being a gentleman after producing in 1700 *The Way of the World*, the most sparkling comedy of manners known to the language.

That such a darkness had settled for many lean and dreary years, few will deny. The blackout was not complete, but it was oppressive. The moralists had snuffed out the candles which burned so brightly in the decades following the Restoration. Gentility had downed audacity, sentiment replaced wit, and romance become the substitute for disenchantment. The characters, who in Lamb's phrase had got out of Christendom into the land of cuckoldry, had returned to Christendom, forsaking that 'Utopia of Gallantry' for a parish of some propriety.

Certainly Goldsmith, when he turned dramatist, first, with *The Good-Natured Man* (1768) and, then, with *She Stoops to Conquer* (1773), did not write in the manner of Etherege, Wycherley, or Congreve. By temperament and endowment he belonged to, and spoke for, an age of greater decorum. He was light-hearted, easy-going, and genial. He was more humorous than witty, and a *farceur* rather than a comic dramatist. It is somewhat in the Goldsmith tradition that Sheridan, in spite of being a worldling, started his career when he wrote *The Rivals*. The proof of his astonishing growth is that within a short two years Sheridan was able, although like Goldsmith the product of the changed values of his times, to write in *The School for Scandal* the play which comes closer than any other later work to Congreve's masterpiece.

The dialogue in *The School for Scandal* may lack the final subtlety and texture of that in *The Way of the World*. The comedy may, as Louis Kronenberger has pointed out in *The Thread of Laughter*, be concerned with 'the imputation of sin' while 'of sin itself there is absolutely nothing'. Yet its scandal-mongers are devastating in their malice; its characters are brilliantly drawn; its observation of society is witty and merciless; Sir Peter and Lady Teazle are two mismated tongue-waggers whose parryings are in the great tradition; and its famous 'screen scene' remains even now, when unfortified by surprise, a triumphant proof of Sheridan's mastery of stagecraft.

To say that *The Rivals* is a far more innocent comedy, much kinder in its spirit and infinitely simpler in the sources of its amusement, is not to deny its merits. These are as unmistakable as its appeal. So knowing is it in the ways and devices of the stage that it is still astonishing to remember it was the work of a young man who insisted he was 'by no means conversant with plays in general either in reading or at the theatre'.

There are echoes in *The Rivals*, plenty of them, because Sheridan knew more about the theatre than he cared to admit. Nonetheless Sheridan already had a voice of his own. A touch, too. Accordingly, when he made use of the tried and the familiar, he altered or extended them in so fresh and personal a way that the old seems new and the hackneyed acquires the illusion of novelty.

It is not necessary to be a rodent of research to realize that, when Mrs. Malaprop does damage to the dictionary, she is proving that the blood of Dogberry flows in her veins; or to remember that, when the quaking Bob Acres is coerced into a duel, he is following in the footsteps of such earlier stage cowards as Sir Andrew Aguecheek. It is equally easy to spot the other conventional comic dodges which Sheridan presses into service and to note that his characters are types, graduates of 'the comedy of humor', each the expression of an outstanding trait, and all oversimplified and blown up large.

But *The Rivals* has never suffered in performance because of these aspects in its writing which win the frowns of intellectuals whose search is only for comedy at its highest. In fact, one of the reasons for the pleasure it has continued to give over the long years is the skill with which Sheridan manipulates the obvious, a feat quite different from the ease with which he handles the subtle and the sophisticated in *The School for Scandal*.

To contend that *The Rivals* remains a delight throughout, even on its own rough-and-tumble level, would be to lie. Few lovers in stage history are more intolerably dull than Faulkland, and few ladies pursued more pallid than Julia. There are plenty of moments, too, when the farcical machinery puffs and sputters and threatens to come to a stop. Even so, the play deserves the place it has won and held as a stage classic. To catalogue its *genre* of comedy may be hard, but not to enjoy it is harder still.

If in it Sheridan deals with life in Bath, elopements, duels, and romance, it is because he was something of an authority on all these subjects at that time. His family had lived in Bath for several years. He had fallen desperately in love there with the much-courted Elizabeth Ann Linley, eloped with her to France, returned to Bath to fight two bloodless duels with a man who had been forcing his attentions on her, and had recently moved to London with his young wife where he was living in much style, though prophetically beyond his means. In short, when Sheridan wrote *The Rivals*, he wrote as a happy man and his happiness is present in almost every line.

That happiness spills across the footlights and is wonderfully contagious. It is to be found in Sheridan's gentle spoofing of Lydia Languish who is romantic enough to think that an elopement is better than a conventional wedding and to prefer poverty to wealth. It is unmistakable no less in Sir Lucius O'Trigger's blustering spirit than in Bob Acres' colorful repertory of oaths and his trembling approach to danger. And no one can miss it in those grave punishments Mrs. Malaprop inflicts upon the dictionary, which remain fun no matter how tattered they may be from repetition.

The Sheridan who wrote *The Rivals* with a light heart also wrote as a man who was that unusual combination, a writer as well as a playwright. Already there are proofs in his dialogue of the rippling command of language and polished style which were to find full expression in *The School for Scandal*. Perhaps the most amazing feature of *The Rivals* is that so young a person should in his first play show such a certain instinct for the stage. His comedy is filled with parts that actors in generation after generation have found hard to resist.

'The best terms will grow obsolete,' says Bob Acres, explaining his ever-changing oaths. 'Damns have had their day.' Most comedies age with greater speed than oaths and almost as rapidly as journalism. The final tribute to Sheridan's skill is that *The Rivals* is a period piece which, whenever it has been adequately presented, has continued to please hosts of playgoers in the period in which it was revived.

JOHN MASON BROWN

THE AUTHOR'S PREFACE

A PREFACE to a play seems generally to be considered as a kind of closet-prologue, in which—if his piece has been successful—the author solicits that indulgence from the reader which he had before experienced from the audience: but as the scope and immediate object of a play is to please a mixed assembly in *representation* (whose judgment in the theatre at least is decisive), its degree of reputation is usually as determined by the public, before it can be prepared for the cooler tribunal of the study. Thus any further solicitude on the part of the writer becomes unnecessary at least, if not an intrusion: and if the piece has been condemned in the performance, I fear an address to the closet, like an appeal to posterity, is constantly regarded as the procrastination of a suit, from a consciousness of the weakness of the cause. From these considerations, the following comedy would certainly have been submitted to the reader, without any further introduction than what it had in the representation, but that its success has probably been founded on a circumstance which the author is informed has not before attended a theatrical trial, and which consequently ought not to pass unnoticed.

I need scarcely add, that the circumstance alluded to was the withdrawing of the piece, to remove those imperfections in the first representation which were too obvious to escape reprehension, and too numerous to admit of a hasty correction. There are few writers, I believe, who, even in the fullest consciousness of error, do not wish to palliate the faults which they acknowledge; and, however trifling the performance, to second their confession of its deficiencies, by whatever plea seems least disgraceful to their ability. In the present instance, it cannot be said to amount either to candour or modesty in me, to acknowledge an extreme inexperience and want of judgment on matters, in which, without guidance from practice, or spur from success, a young man should scarcely boast of being an adept. If it be said that under such disadvantages no one should attempt to write a play, I must beg leave to dissent from the position, while the first point of experience that I have gained on the subject is, a knowledge of the candour and judgment with which an impartial public distinguishes between the errors of inexperience and incapacity, and the indulgence which it shows even to a disposition to remedy the defects of either.

It were unnecessary to enter into any further extenuation of what was thought exceptionable in this play, but that it has been said, that the managers should have prevented some of the defects before its appearance to the public—and in particular the uncommon length of the piece as represented the first night. It were an ill return for the most liberal and gentlemanly conduct on their side, to suffer any censure to rest where none was deserved. Hurry in writing has long been exploded as an excuse for an author;—however, in the dramatic line, it may happen, that both an author and a manager may wish to fill a chasm in the entertainment of the public with a hastiness not altogether culpable. The season was advanced when I first put the play into Mr. Harris's hands: it was at that time at least double the length of any acting comedy. I profited by his judgment and experience in the curtailing of it—till, I believe, his feeling for the vanity of a young author got the better of his desire for correctness, and he left many excrescences remaining, because he had assisted in pruning so many more. Hence, though I was not uninformed that the acts were still too long, I flattered myself that, after the first trial, I might with safer judgment proceed to remove what should appear to have been most dissatisfactory. Many other errors there were, which might in part have arisen from my being by no means conversant with plays in general, either in reading or at the theatre. Yet I own that, in one respect, I did not regret my ignorance: for as my first wish in attempting a play was to avoid every appearance of plagiary, I thought I should stand a better chance of effecting this from being in a walk which I had not frequented, and where, consequently, the progress of invention was less likely to be interrupted by starts of recollection: for on subjects on which the mind has been much informed, invention is slow of exerting itself. Faded ideas float in the fancy like half-forgotten dreams; and the imagination in its fullest enjoyments becomes suspicious of its offspring, and doubts whether it has created or adopted.

With regard to some particular passages which on the first night's representation seemed generally disliked, I confess that if I felt any emotion of surprise at the disapprobation, it was not that they were disapproved of, but that I had not before perceived that they deserved it. As some part of the attack on the piece was begun too early to pass for the sentence of *judgment*, which is ever tardy in condemning, it has been suggested to me that much of the disapprobation must have arisen from virulence of malice, rather than severity of criticism: but as I was more apprehensive of there being just grounds to excite the latter than conscious of having deserved the former, I continue not to believe that probable which I am sure must have been unprovoked. However, if it was so, and I could even mark the quarter from whence it came, it would be ungenerous to retort; for no passion suffers more than malice from disappointment. For my own part, I see no reason why the author of a play should not regard a first night's audience as a candid and judicious friend attending, in behalf of the public, at his last rehearsal. If he can dispense with flattery, he is sure at least of sincerity, and even though the annotation be rude, he may rely upon the justness of the comment. Considered in this light, that audience, whose *fiat* is essential to the poet's claim, whether his object be fame or profit, has surely a right to expect some deference to its opinion, from principles of politeness at least, if not from gratitude.

As for the little puny critics, who scatter their peevish strictures in private circles, and scribble at every author who has the eminence of being unconnected with them, as they are usually spleen-swoln from a vain idea of increasing their consequence, there will always be found a petulance and illiberality in their remarks, which should place them as far beneath the notice of a gentleman as their original dulness had sunk them from the level of the most unsuccessful author.

It is not without pleasure that I catch at an opportunity of justifying myself from the charge of intending any national

16

reflection in the character of Sir Lucius O'Trigger. If any gentlemen opposed the piece from that idea, I thank them sincerely for their opposition; and if the condemnation of this comedy (however misconceived the provocation) could have added one spark to the decaying flame of national attachment to the country supposed to be reflected on, I should have been happy in its fate, and might with truth have boasted that it had done more real service in its failure than the successful morality of a thousand stage-novels will ever effect.

It is usual, I believe, to thank the performers in a new play for the exertion of their several abilities. But where (as in this instance) their merit has been so striking and uncontroverted as to call for the warmest and truest applause from a number of judicious audiences, the poet's after-praise comes like the feeble acclamation of a child to close the shouts of a multitude. The conduct, however, of the principals in a theatre cannot be so apparent to the public. I think it therefore but justice to declare, that from this theatre (the only one I can speak of from experience) those writers who wish to try the dramatic line will meet with that candour and liberal attention which are generally allowed to be better calculated to lead genius into excellence than either the precepts of judgment or the guidance of experience.

THE AUTHOR

B

THE FIRST PROLOGUE

SPOKEN BY MR. WOODWARD AND MR. QUICK

Enter SERJEANT-AT-LAW, *and* ATTORNEY
following, and giving a paper

SERJEANT-AT-LAW
What's here!—a vile cramp hand! I cannot see
Without my spectacles.

ATTORNEY

He means his fee.
Nay, Mr. Serjeant, good sir, try again. [*Gives money*.

SERJEANT-AT-LAW
The scrawl improves! [*more*] O come, 'tis pretty plain.
Hey! how's this? Dibble!—sure it cannot be!
A poet's brief! a poet and a fee!

ATTORNEY
Yes, sir! though you without reward, I know,
Would gladly plead the Muse's cause.

SERJEANT-AT-LAW

So!—So!

ATTORNEY
And if the fee offends, your wrath should fall
On me.

SERJEANT-AT-LAW
Dear Dibble, no offence at all.

ATTORNEY

Some sons of Phœbus in the courts we meet,

SERJEANT-AT-LAW

And fifty sons of Phœbus in the Fleet!

ATTORNEY

Nor pleads he worse, who with a decent sprig
Of bays adorns his legal waste of wig.

SERJEANT-AT-LAW

Full-bottomed heroes thus, on signs, unfurl
A leaf of laurel in a grove of curl!
Yet tell your client, that, in adverse days,
This wig is warmer than a bush of bays.

ATTORNEY

Do you, then, sir, my client's place supply,
Profuse of robe, and prodigal of tie——
Do you, with all those blushing powers of face,
And wonted bashful hesitating grace,
Rise in the court and flourish on the case.   [*Exit.*

SERJEANT-AT-LAW

For practice then suppose—this brief will show it,—
Me, Serjeant Woodward,—counsel for the poet.
Used to the ground, I know 'tis hard to deal
With this dread court, from whence there's no appeal;
No tricking here, to blunt the edge of law,
Or, damn'd in equity, escape by flaw:
But judgment given, your sentence must remain;
No writ of error lies—to Drury-lane!
   Yet when so kind you seem, 'tis past dispute
We gain some favour, if not costs of suit.
No spleen is here! I see no hoarded fury;—
I think I never faced a milder jury!

Sad else our plight! where frowns are transportation,
A hiss the gallows, and a groan damnation!
But such the public candour, without fear
My client waives all right of challenge here.
No newsman from our session is dismiss'd,
Nor wit nor critic we scratch off the list;
His faults can never hurt another's ease,
His crime, at worst, a bad attempt to please:
Thus, all respecting, he appeals to all,
And by the general voice will stand or fall.

THE SECOND PROLOGUE

SPOKEN ON THE TENTH NIGHT
BY MRS. BULKLEY

GRANTED our cause, our suit and trial o'er,
The worthy serjeant need appear no more:
In pleasing I a different client choose,
He served the Poet—I would serve the Muse.
Like him, I'll try to merit your applause,
A female counsel in a female's cause.
    Look on this form,[1]—where humour, quaint and sly,
Dimples the cheek, and points the beaming eye;
Where gay invention seems to boast its wiles
In amorous hint, and half-triumphant smiles;
While her light mask or covers satire's strokes,
Or hides the conscious blush her wit provokes.
Look on her well—does she seem form'd to teach?

[1]Pointing to the figure of Comedy.

Should you expect to hear this lady preach?
Is grey experience suited to her youth?
Do solemn sentiments become that mouth?
Bid her be grave, those lips should rebel prove
To every theme that slanders mirth or love.

    Yet, thus adorn'd with every graceful art
To charm the fancy and yet reach the heart——
Must we displace her, and instead advance
The goddess of the woful countenance—
The sentimental Muse?—Her emblems view,
The Pilgrim's Progress, and a sprig of rue!
View her—too chaste to look like flesh and blood—
Primly portray'd on emblematic wood!
There, fix'd in usurpation, should she stand,
She'll snatch the dagger from her sister's hand:
And having made her votaries weep a flood,
Good heaven! she'll end her comedies in blood—
Bid Harry Woodward break poor Dunstal's crown
Imprison Quick, and knock Ned Shuter down;
While sad Barsanti, weeping o'er the scene,
Shall stab herself—or poison Mrs. Green.

    Such dire encroachments to prevent in time,
Demands the critic's voice—the poet's rhyme.
Can our light scenes add strength to holy laws!
Such puny patronage but hurts the cause:
Fair virtue scorns our feeble aid to ask;
And moral truth disdains the trickster's mask.
For here their favourite stands,[1] whose brow, severe
And sad, claims youth's respect, and pity's tear;
Who, when oppress'd by foes her worth creates,
Can point a poniard at the guilt she hates.

[1]Pointing to Tragedy.

21

DRAMATIS PERSONÆ

AS ORIGINALLY ACTED AT COVENT-GARDEN
THEATRE IN 1775

SIR ANTHONY ABSOLUTE   *Mr. Shuter*
CAPTAIN ABSOLUTE   *Mr. Woodward*
FAULKLAND   *Mr. Lewis*
ACRES   *Mr. Quick*
SIR LUCIUS O'TRIGGER   *Mr. Lee*
FAG   *Mr. Lee Lewes*
DAVID   *Mr. Dunstal*
THOMAS   *Mr. Fearon*
MRS. MALAPROP   *Mrs. Green*
LYDIA LANGUISH   *Miss Barsanti*
JULIA   *Mrs. Bulkley*
LUCY   *Mrs. Lessingham*

Maid, Boy, Servants, &c.

SCENE: BATH

Time of Action—Five Hours

ACT ONE

SCENE ONE

A Street

Enter THOMAS; *he crosses the Stage;*
FAG *follows, looking after him*

FAG

What! Thomas! Sure 'tis he?—What! Thomas!
Thomas!

THOMAS

Hey!—Odd's life! Mr. Fag!—give us your hand, my
old fellow-servant.

FAG

Excuse my glove, Thomas:—I'm devilish glad to see
you, my lad. Why, my prince of charioteers, you look
as hearty!—but who the deuce thought of seeing you
in Bath?

THOMAS

Sure, master, Madam Julia, Harry, Mrs. Kate, and
the postilion, be all come.

FAG

Indeed!

THOMAS

Ay, master thought another fit of the gout was coming
to make him a visit; so he'd a mind to gi't the slip, and
whip! we were all off at an hour's warning.

23

FAG

Ay, ay, hasty in everything, or it would not be Sir Anthony Absolute!

THOMAS

But tell us, Mr. Fag, how does young master? Odd! Sir Anthony will stare to see the captain here!

FAG

I do not serve Captain Absolute now.

THOMAS

Why sure!

FAG

At present I am employed by Ensign Beverley.

THOMAS

I doubt, Mr. Fag, you ha'n't changed for the better.

FAG

I have not changed, Thomas.

THOMAS

No! Why didn't you say you had left young master?

FAG

No.—Well, honest Thomas, I must puzzle you no farther:—briefly then—Captain Absolute and Ensign Beverley are one and the same person.

THOMAS

The devil they are!

FAG

So it is indeed, Thomas; and the ensign half of my master being on guard at present—the captain has nothing to do with me.

THOMAS

So, so!—What, this is some freak, I warrant!—Do

THOMAS

tell us, Mr. Fag, the meaning o't—you know I ha' trusted you.

FAG

You'll be secret, Thomas?

THOMAS

As a coach-horse.

FAG

Why then the cause of all this is—Love,—Love, Thomas, who (as you may get read to you) has been a masquerader ever since the days of Jupiter.

THOMAS

Ay, ay;—I guessed there was a lady in the case:—but pray, why does your master pass only for an ensign? —Now if he had shammed general indeed——

FAG

Ah! Thomas, there lies the mystery o' the matter. Hark'ee, Thomas, my master is in love with a lady of a very singular taste: a lady who likes him better as a half-pay ensign than if she knew he was son and heir to Sir Anthony Absolute, a baronet of three thousand a year.

THOMAS

That is an odd taste indeed!—But has she got the stuff, Mr. Fag? Is she rich, hey?

FAG

Rich!—Why, I believe she owns half the stocks! Zounds! Thomas, she could pay the national debt as easily as I could my washerwoman! She has a lap-dog that eats out of gold,—she feeds her parrot with small pearls,—and all her thread-papers are made of banknotes!

THOMAS

Bravo, faith!—Odd! I warrant she has a set of thousands at least:—but does she draw kindly with the captain?

FAG

As fond as pigeons.

THOMAS

May one hear her name?

FAG

Miss Lydia Languish.—But there is an old tough aunt in the way; though, by-the-by, she has never seen my master—for we got acquainted with miss while on a visit in Gloucestershire.

THOMAS

Well—I wish they were once harnessed together in matrimony.—But pray, Mr. Fag, what kind of a place is this Bath?—I ha' heard a deal of it—here's a mort o' merry-making, hey?

FAG

Pretty well, Thomas, pretty well—'tis a good lounge; in the morning we go to the pump-room (though neither my master nor I drink the waters); after breakfast we saunter on the parades, or play a game at billiards; at night we dance; but damn the place, I'm tired of it: their regular hours stupefy me—not a fiddle nor a card after eleven!—However, Mr. Faulkland's gentleman and I keep it up a little in private parties;—I'll introduce you there, Thomas— you'll like him much.

THOMAS

Sure I know Mr. Du-Peigne—you know his master is to marry Madam Julia.

26

FAG

I had forgot.—But, Thomas, you must polish a little
—indeed you must.—Here now—this wig! What the
devil do you do with a wig, Thomas?—None of the
London whips of any degree of *ton* wear wigs now.

THOMAS

More's the pity! more's the pity! I say.—Odd's life!
when I heard how the lawyers and doctors had took
to their own hair, I thought how 'twould go next:—
odd rabbit it! when the fashion had got foot on the
bar, I guessed 'twould mount to the box!—but 'tis all
out of character, believe me, Mr. Fag: and look'ee,
I'll never gi' up mine—the lawyers and doctors may
do as they will.

FAG

Well, Thomas, we'll not quarrel about that.

THOMAS

Why, bless you, the gentlemen of the professions
ben't all of a mind—for in our village now, thoff Jack
Gauge, the exciseman, has ta'en to his carrots, there's
little Dick the farrier swears he'll never forsake his
bob, though all the college should appear with their
own heads!

FAG

Indeed! well said, Dick!—but hold—mark! mark!
Thomas.

THOMAS

Zooks! 'tis the captain.—Is that the Lady with him?

FAG

No, no, that is Madam Lucy, my master's mistress's
maid. They lodge at that house—but I must after him
to tell him the news.

THOMAS

Odd! he's given her money!—Well, Mr. Fag——

FAG

Good-bye, Thomas. I have an appointment in Gyde's porch this evening at eight; meet me there, and we'll make a little party.   [*Exeunt severally.*

SCENE TWO

A Dressing-room in MRS. MALAPROP'S *Lodgings*

LYDIA *sitting on a sofa, with a book in her hand.*
LUCY, *as just returned from a message*

LUCY

Indeed, ma'am, I traversed half the town in search of it! I don't believe there's a circulating library in Bath I han't been at.

LYDIA

And could not you get *The Reward of Constancy?*

LUCY

No, indeed, ma'am.

LYDIA

Nor *The Fatal Connexion?*

LUCY

No, indeed, ma'am.

LYDIA

Nor *The Mistakes of the Heart?*

LUCY

Ma'am, as ill luck would have it, Mr. Bull said Miss Sukey Saunter had just fetched it away.

28

LYDIA

Heigh-ho! Did you inquire for *The Delicate Distress*?

LUCY

Or, *The Memoirs of Lady Woodford*? Yes, indeed, ma'am. I asked everywhere for it; and I might have brought it from Mr. Frederick's, but Lady Slattern Lounger, who had just sent it home, had so soiled and dog's-eared it, it wa'n't fit for a Christian to read.

LYDIA

Heigh-ho! Yes, I always know when Lady Slattern has been before me. She has a most observing thumb; and, I believe, cherishes her nails for the convenience of making marginal notes.—Well, child, what have you brought me?

LUCY

Oh! here, ma'am.—[*Taking books from under her cloak and from her pockets.*] This is *The Gordian Knot*,—and this *Peregrine Pickle*. Here are *The Tears of Sensibility*, and *Humphrey Clinker*. This is *The Memoirs of a Lady of Quality, written by Herself*, and here the second volume of *The Sentimental Journey*.

LYDIA

Heigh-ho!—What are those books by the glass?

LUCY

The great one is only *The Whole Duty of Man*, where I press a few blonds, ma'am.

LYDIA

Very well—give me the sal volatile.

LUCY

Is it in a blue cover, ma'am?

LYDIA

My smelling-bottle, you simpleton!

LUCY

Oh, the drops—here, ma'am.

LYDIA

Hold!—here's some one coming—quick! see who it is.—

[*Exit* LUCY.]

Surely I heard my cousin Julia's voice.

Re-enter LUCY

LUCY

Lud! ma'am, here is Miss Melville.

LYDIA

Is it possible?—   [*Exit* LUCY.

Enter JULIA

LYDIA

My dearest Julia, how delighted am I!—[*Embrace.*] How unexpected was this happiness!

JULIA

True, Lydia—and our pleasure is the greater.—But what has been the matter?—you were denied to me at first!

LYDIA

Ah, Julia, I have a thousand things to tell you!—But first inform me what has conjured you to Bath?—Is Sir Anthony here?

JULIA

He is—we are arrived within this hour—and I suppose he will be here to wait on Mrs. Malaprop as soon as he is dressed.

LYDIA

Then before we are interrupted, let me impart to you

some of my distress!—I know your gentle nature will sympathize with me, though your prudence may condemn me! My letters have informed you of my whole connection with Beverley; but I have lost him, Julia! My aunt has discovered our intercourse by a note she intercepted, and has confined me ever since! Yet, would you believe it? she has absolutely fallen in love with a tall Irish baronet she met one night since she has been here, at Lady Macshuffle's rout.

JULIA

You jest, Lydia!

LYDIA

No, upon my word.—She really carries on a kind of correspondence with him, under a feigned name though, till she chooses to be known to him: but it is a Delia or a Celia, I assure you.

JULIA

Then, surely, she is now more indulgent to her niece.

LYDIA

Quite the contrary. Since she has discovered her own frailty, she is become more suspicious of mine. Then I must inform you of another plague! That odious Acres is to be in Bath to-day: so that I protest I shall be teased out of all spirits!

JULIA

Come, come, Lydia, hope for the best—Sir Anthony shall use his interest with Mrs. Malaprop.

LYDIA

But you have not heard the worst. Unfortunately I had quarrelled with my poor Beverley, just before my aunt made the discovery, and I have not seen him since to make it up.

JULIA

What was his offence?

LYDIA

Nothing at all! But, I don't know how it was, as often as we had been together, we had never had a quarrel, and, somehow, I was afraid he would never give me an opportunity. So, last Thursday, I wrote a letter to myself, to inform myself that Beverley was at that time paying his addresses to another woman. I signed it *your friend unknown*, showed it to Beverley, charged him with his falsehood, put myself in a violent passion, and vowed I'd never see him more.

JULIA

And you let him depart so, and have not seen him since?

LYDIA

'Twas the next day my aunt found the matter out. I intended only to have teased him three days and a half, and now I've lost him for ever.

JULIA

If he is as deserving and sincere as you have represented him to me, he will never give you up so. Yet, consider, Lydia, you tell me he is but an ensign, and you have thirty thousand pounds.

LYDIA

But you know I lose most of my fortune if I marry without my aunt's consent, till of age; and that is what I have determined to do, ever since I knew the penalty. Nor could I love the man who would wish to wait a day for the alternative.

F A G

JULIA

. Nay, this is caprice!

LYDIA

What, does Julia tax me with caprice? I thought her lover Faulkland had inured her to it.

JULIA

I do not love even his faults.

LYDIA

But àpropos—you have sent to him, I suppose?

JULIA

Not yet, upon my word—nor has he the least idea of my being in Bath. Sir Anthony's resolution was so sudden, I could not inform him of it.

LYDIA

Well, Julia, you are your own mistress (though under the protection of Sir Anthony), yet have you, for this long year, been a slave to the caprice, the whim, the jealousy of this ungrateful Faulkland, who will ever delay assuming the right of a husband, while you suffer him to be equally imperious as a lover.

JULIA

Nay, you are wrong entirely. We were contracted before my father's death. That, and some consequent embarrassments, have delayed what I know to be my Faulkland's most ardent wish. He is too generous to trifle on such a point—and for his character, you wrong him there, too. No, Lydia, he is too proud, too noble, to be jealous; if he is captious, 'tis without dissembling; if fretful, without rudeness. Unused to the fopperies of love, he is negligent of the little duties expected from a lover—but being unhackneyed in the

D   33

passion, his affection is ardent and sincere; and as it engrosses his whole soul, he expects every thought and emotion of his mistress to move in unison with his. Yet, though his pride calls for this full return, his humility makes him undervalue those qualities in him which would entitle him to it; and not feeling why he should be loved to the degree he wishes, he still suspects that he is not loved enough. This temper, I must own, has cost me many unhappy hours; but I have learned to think myself his debtor, for those imperfections which arise from the ardour of his attachment.

LYDIA

Well, I cannot blame you for defending him. But tell me candidly, Julia, had he never saved your life, do you think you should have been attached to him as you are?—Believe me, the rude blast that overset your boat was a prosperous gale of love to him.

JULIA

Gratitude may have strengthened my attachment to Mr. Faulkland, but I loved him before he had preserved me; yet surely that alone were an obligation sufficient.

LYDIA

Obligation! why a water spaniel would have done as much!—Well, I should never think of giving my heart to a man because he could swim.

JULIA

Come, Lydia, you are too inconsiderate.

LYDIA

Nay, I do but jest—What's here?

Re-enter LUCY *in a hurry*

34

LUCY

O ma'am, here is Sir Anthony Absolute just come home with your aunt.

LYDIA

They'll not come here.—Lucy, do you watch.

[*Exit* LUCY.

JULIA

Yet I must go. Sir Anthony does not know I am here, and if we meet, he'll detain me, to show me the town. I'll take another opportunity of paying my respects to Mrs. Malaprop, when she shall treat me, as long as she chooses, with her select words so ingeniously misapplied, without being mispronounced.

Re-enter LUCY

LUCY

O Lud! ma'am, they are both coming upstairs.

LYDIA

Well, I'll not detain you, coz.—Adieu, my dear Julia. I'm sure you are in haste to send to Faulkland.— There, through my room you'll find another staircase.

JULIA

Adieu! [*Embraces* LYDIA, *and exit.*

LYDIA

Here, my dear Lucy, hide these books. Quick, quick! —Fling *Peregrine Pickle* under the toilet—throw *Roderick Random* into the closet—put *The Innocent Adultery* into *The Whole Duty of Man*—thrust *Lord Aimworth* under the sofa—cram *Ovid* behind the bolster—there—put *The Man of Feeling* into your pocket—so, so—now lay *Mrs. Chapone* in sight, and leave *Fordyce's Sermons* open on the table.

35

LUCY

O burn it, ma'am! the hair-dresser has torn away as far as *Proper Pride*.

LYDIA

Never mind—open at *Sobriety*.—Fling me *Lord Chesterfield's Letters*. Now for 'em.   [*Exit* LUCY.

Enter MRS. MALAPROP *and* SIR ANTHONY
ABSOLUTE

MRS. MALAPROP

There, Sir Anthony, there sits the deliberate simpleton who wants to disgrace her family, and lavish herself on a fellow not worth a shilling.

LYDIA

Madam, I thought you once—

MRS. MALAPROP

You thought, miss! I don't know any business you have to think at all—thought does not become a young woman. But the point we would request of you is, that you will promise to forget this fellow—to illiterate him, I say, quite from your memory.

LYDIA

Ah, madam! our memories are independent of our wills. It is not so easy to forget.

MRS. MALAPROP

But I say it is, miss; there is nothing on earth so easy as to forget, if a person chooses to set about it. I'm sure I have as much forgot your poor dear uncle as if he had never existed—and I thought it my duty so to do; and let me tell you, Lydia, these violent memories don't become a young woman.

SIR ANTHONY

Why sure she won't pretend to remember what she's ordered not!—ay, this comes of her reading!

LYDIA

What crime, madam, have I committed, to be treated thus?

MRS. MALAPROP

Now don't attempt to extirpate yourself from the matter; you know I have proof controvertible of it. —But tell me, will you promise to do as you're bid? Will you take a husband of your friends' choosing?

LYDIA

Madam, I must tell you plainly, that had I no preference for any one else, the choice you have made would be my aversion.

MRS. MALAPROP

What business have you, miss, with preference and aversion? They don't become a young woman; and you ought to know, that as both always wear off, 'tis safest in matrimony to begin with a little aversion. I am sure I hated your poor dear uncle before marriage as if he'd been a blackamoor—and yet, miss, you are sensible what a wife I made!—and when it pleased Heaven to release me from him, 'tis unknown what tears I shed! But suppose we were going to give you another choice, will you promise us to give up this Beverley?

LYDIA

Could I belie my thoughts so far as to give that promise, my actions would certainly as far belie my words.

37

MRS. MALAPROP

Take yourself to your room. You are fit company for nothing but your own ill-humours.

LYDIA

Willingly, ma'am—I cannot change for the worse.

[*Exit.*

MRS. MALAPROP

There's a little intricate hussy for you!

SIR ANTHONY

It is not to be wondered at, ma'am,—all this is the natural consequence of teaching girls to read. Had I a thousand daughters, by Heaven! I'd as soon have them taught the black art as their alphabet!

MRS. MALAPROP

Nay, nay, Sir Anthony, you are an absolute misanthropy.

SIR ANTHONY

In my way hither, Mrs. Malaprop, I observed your niece's maid coming forth from a circulating library! —She had a book in each hand—they were half-bound volumes, with marble covers!—From that moment I guessed how full of duty I should see her mistress!

MRS. MALAPROP

Those are vile places, indeed!

SIR ANTHONY

Madam, a circulating library in a town is as an evergreen tree of diabolical knowledge! It blossoms through the year!—and depend on it, Mrs. Malaprop, that they who are so fond of handling the leaves, will long for the fruit at last.

38

MRS. MALAPROP

Fy, fy, Sir Anthony, you surely speak laconically.

SIR ANTHONY

Why, Mrs. Malaprop, in moderation now, what would you have a woman know?

MRS. MALAPROP

Observe me, Sir Anthony. I would by no means wish a daughter of mine to be a progeny of learning; I don't think so much learning becomes a young woman; for instance, I would never let her meddle with Greek, or Hebrew, or algebra, or simony, or fluxions, or paradoxes, or such inflammatory branches of learning—neither would it be necessary for her to handle any of your mathematical, astronomical, diabolical instruments.—But, Sir Anthony, I would send her, at nine years old, to a boarding-school, in order to learn a little ingenuity and artifice. Then, sir, she should have a supercilious knowledge in accounts;—and as she grew up, I would have her instructed in geometry, that she might know something of the contagious countries;—but above all, Sir Anthony, she should be mistress of orthodoxy, that she might not mis-spell, and mis-pronounce words, so shamefully as girls usually do; and likewise that she might reprehend the true meaning of what she is saying. This, Sir Anthony, is what I would have a woman know—and I don't think there is a superstitious article in it.

SIR ANTHONY

Well, well, Mrs. Malaprop, I will dispute the point no further with you; though I must confess that you are a truly moderate and polite arguer, for almost every third word you say is on my side of the question. But, Mrs. Malaprop, to the more important point in debate—you say you have no objection to my proposal?

MRS. MALAPROP

None, I assure you. I am under no positive engagement with Mr. Acres, and as Lydia is so obstinate against him, perhaps your son may have better success.

SIR ANTHONY

Well, madam, I will write for the boy directly. He knows not a syllable of this yet, though I have for some time had the proposal in my head. He is at present with his regiment.

MRS. MALAPROP

We have never seen your son, Sir Anthony; but I hope no objection on his side.

SIR ANTHONY

Objection!—let him object if he dare!—No, no, Mrs. Malaprop, Jack knows that the least demur puts me in a frenzy directly. My process was always very simple—in their younger days, 'twas 'Jack do this';— if he demurred, I knocked him down—and if he grumbled at that, I always sent him out of the room.

MRS. MALAPROP

Ah, and the properest way, o' my conscience!— nothing is so conciliating to young people as severity. —Well, Sir Anthony, I shall give Mr. Acres his discharge, and prepare Lydia to receive your son's invocations;—and I hope you will represent her to the captain as an object not altogether illegible.

SIR ANTHONY

Madam, I will handle the subject prudently.—Well, I must leave you; and let me beg you, Mrs. Malaprop, to enforce this matter roundly to the girl.—Take my advice—keep a tight hand; if she rejects this proposal, clap her under lock and key; and if you were just to let the servants forget to bring her dinner for three or four days, you can't conceive how she'd come about.

[*Exit.*

MRS. MALAPROP

Well, at any rate, I shall be glad to get her from under my intuition. She has somehow discovered my partiality for Sir Lucius O'Trigger—sure, Lucy can't have betrayed me!—No, the girl is such a simpleton, I should have made her confess it.—Lucy!—Lucy! —[*Calls.*] Had she been one of your artificial ones, I should never have trusted her.

Re-enter LUCY

LUCY

Did you call, ma'am?

MRS. MALAPROP

Yes, girl.—Did you see Sir Lucius while you was out?

LUCY

No, indeed, ma'am, not a glimpse of him.

MRS. MALAPROP

You are sure, Lucy, that you never mentioned——

LUCY

Oh, gemini! I'd sooner cut my tongue out.

MRS. MALAPROP

Well, don't let your simplicity be imposed on.

LUCY

No, ma'am.

MRS. MALAPROP

So, come to me presently, and I'll give you another letter to Sir Lucius; but mind, Lucy—if ever you betray what you are entrusted with (unless it be other people's secrets to me), you forfeit my malevolence for ever, and your being a simpleton shall be no excuse for your locality. [*Exit.*

LUCY

Ha! ha! ha!—So, my dear Simplicity, let me give you a little respite.—[*Altering her manner.*] Let girls in my station be as fond as they please of appearing expert, and knowing in their trusts; commend me to a mask of silliness, and a pair of sharp eyes for my own interest under it!—Let me see to what account have I turned my simplicity lately.—[*Looks at a paper.*] For *abetting Miss Lydia Languish in a design of running away with an ensign!—in money, sundry times, twelve pound twelve; gowns, five; hats, ruffles, caps, etc., etc., numberless!— From the said ensign, within this last month, six guineas and a half.*—About a quarter's pay!—Item, *from Mrs. Malaprop, for betraying the young people to her*—when I found matters were likely to be discovered—*two guineas and a black paduasoy.*—Item, *from Mr. Acres, for carrying divers letters*—which I never delivered— *two guineas and a pair of buckles*—Item, *from Sir Lucius O'Trigger, three crowns, two gold pocket-pieces, and a silver snuff-box!*—Well done, Simplicity!—Yet I was forced to make my Hibernian believe that he was corresponding, not with the aunt, but with the niece; for though not over rich, I found he had too much pride and delicacy to sacrifice the feelings of a gentleman to the necessities of his fortune. [*Exit.*

ACT TWO

SCENE ONE

CAPTAIN ABSOLUTE'S *Lodgings*

CAPTAIN ABSOLUTE *and* FAG

FAG

Sir, while I was there, Sir Anthony came in: I told him you had sent me to inquire after his health, and to know if he was at leisure to see you.

CAPTAIN ABSOLUTE

And what did he say, on hearing I was at Bath?

FAG

Sir, in my life I never saw an elderly gentleman more astonished! He started back two or three paces, rapped out a dozen interjectural oaths, and asked what the devil had brought you here.

CAPTAIN ABSOLUTE

Well, sir, and what did you say?

FAG

Oh, I lied, sir—I forget the precise lie; but you may depend on't, he got no truth from me. Yet, with submission, for fear of blunders in future, I should be glad to fix what has brought us to Bath, in order that we may lie a little consistently. Sir Anthony's servants were curious, sir, very curious indeed.

43

CAPTAIN ABSOLUTE

You have said nothing to them?

FAG

Oh, not a word, sir,—not a word! Mr. Thomas, indeed, the coachman (whom I take to be the discreetest of whips)——

CAPTAIN ABSOLUTE

'Sdeath!—you rascal! you have not trusted him!

FAG

Oh, no, sir—no—no—not a syllable, upon my veracity!—He was, indeed, a little inquisitive; but I was sly, sir—devilish sly! My master (said I), honest Thomas (you know, sir, one says honest to one's inferiors), is come to Bath to recruit.—Yes, sir, I said to recruit—and whether for men, money, or constitution, you know, sir, is nothing to him nor any one else.

CAPTAIN ABSOLUTE

Well, recruit will do—let it be so.

FAG

Oh, sir, recruit will do surprisingly—indeed, to give the thing an air, I told Thomas that your honour had already enlisted five disbanded chairmen, seven minority waiters, and thirteen billiard-markers.

CAPTAIN ABSOLUTE

You blockhead, never say more than is necessary.

FAG

I beg pardon, sir—I beg pardon—but, with submission, a lie is nothing unless one supports it. Sir, whenever I draw on my invention for a good current lie, I always forge indorsements as well as the bill.

44

CAPTAIN ABSOLUTE

Well, take care you don't hurt your credit by offering too much security.—Is Mr. Faulkland returned?

FAG

He is above, sir, changing his dress.

CAPTAIN ABSOLUTE

Can you tell whether he has been informed of Sir Anthony and Miss Melville's arrival?

FAG

I fancy not, sir; he has seen no one since he came in but his gentleman, who was with him at Bristol.—I think, sir, I hear Mr. Faulkland coming down——

CAPTAIN ABSOLUTE

Go tell him I am here.

FAG

Yes, sir.—[*Going.*] I beg pardon, sir, but should Sir Anthony call, you will do me the favour to remember that we are recruiting, if you please.

CAPTAIN ABSOLUTE

Well, well.

FAG

And, in tenderness to my character, if your honour could bring in the chairmen and waiters, I should esteem it as an obligation; for though I never scruple a lie to serve my master, yet it hurts one's conscience to be found out.   [*Exit.*

CAPTAIN ABSOLUTE

Now for my whimsical friend—if he does not know that his mistress is here, I'll tease him a little before I tell him——

Enter FAULKLAND

45

Faulkland, you're welcome to Bath again; you are punctual in your return.

FAULKLAND

Yes; I had nothing to detain me when I had finished the business I went on. Well, what news since I left you? how stand matters between you and Lydia?

CAPTAIN ABSOLUTE

Faith, much as they were; I have not seen her since our quarrel; however, I expect to be recalled every hour.

FAULKLAND

Why don't you persuade her to go off with you at once?

CAPTAIN ABSOLUTE

What, and lose two-thirds of her fortune? You forget that, my friend.—No, no, I could have brought her to that long ago.

FAULKLAND

Nay, then, you trifle too long—if you are sure of her, propose to the aunt in your own character, and write to Sir Anthony for his consent.

CAPTAIN ABSOLUTE

Softly, softly; for though I am convinced my little Lydia would elope with me as Ensign Beverley, yet am I by no means certain that she would take me with the impediment of our friends' consent, a regular humdrum wedding, and the reversion of a good fortune on my side: no, no; I must prepare her gradually for the discovery, and make myself necessary to her, before I risk it.—Well, but Faulkland; you'll dine with us to-day at the hotel?

46

FAULKLAND

Indeed, I cannot; I am not in spirits to be of such a party.

CAPTAIN ABSOLUTE

By heavens! I shall forswear your company. You are the most teasing, captious, incorrigible lover!—Do love like a man.

FAULKLAND

I own I am unfit for company.

CAPTAIN ABSOLUTE

Am I not a lover; ay, and a romantic one too? Yet do I carry everywhere with me such a confounded farrago of doubts, fears, hopes, wishes, and all the flimsy furniture of a country miss's brain!

FAULKLAND

Ah! Jack, your heart and soul are not, like mine, fixed immutably on one only object. You throw for a large stake, but losing, you could stake and throw again:— but I have set my sum of happiness on this cast, and not to succeed were to be stripped of all.

CAPTAIN ABSOLUTE

But, for heaven's sake! what grounds for apprehension can your whimsical brain conjure up at present?

FAULKLAND

What grounds for apprehension, did you say? Heavens! are there not a thousand! I fear for her spirits—her health—her life!—My absence may fret her; her anxiety for my return, her fears for me, may oppress her gentle temper: and for her health, does not every hour bring me cause to be alarmed? If it rains, some shower may even then have chilled her delicate frame! If the wind be keen, some rude blast may have affected her! The heat of noon, the dews of the evening, may endanger the life of her for whom only I value mine. O Jack! when delicate and feeling souls are separated, there is not a feature in the sky, not a movement of the elements, not an aspiration of the breeze, but hints some cause for a lover's apprehension!

CAPTAIN ABSOLUTE

Ay, but we may choose whether we will take the hint or not.—So, then, Faulkland, if you were convinced that Julia were well and in spirits, you would be entirely content?

FAULKLAND

I should be happy beyond measure—I am anxious only for that.

CAPTAIN ABSOLUTE

Then to cure your anxiety at once—Miss Melville is in perfect health, and is at this moment in Bath.

FAULKLAND

Nay, Jack—don't trifle with me.

CAPTAIN ABSOLUTE

She is arrived here with my father within this hour.

FAULKLAND

Can you be serious?

CAPTAIN ABSOLUTE

I thought you knew Sir Anthony better than to be surprised at a sudden whim of this kind.—Seriously, then, it is as I tell you—upon my honour.

FAULKLAND

My dear friend!—Hollo, Du-Peigne! my hat.—My

LUCY

dear Jack—now nothing on earth can give me a moment's uneasiness.

Re-enter FAG

FAG

Sir, Mr. Acres, just arrived, is below.

CAPTAIN ABSOLUTE

Stay, Faulkland, this Acres lives within a mile of Sir Anthony, and he shall tell you how your mistress has been ever since you left her. Fag, show this gentleman up.   [*Exit* FAG.

FAULKLAND

What, is he much acquainted in the family?

CAPTAIN ABSOLUTE

Oh, very intimate: I insist on your not going: besides, his character will divert you.

FAULKLAND

Well, I should like to ask him a few questions.

CAPTAIN ABSOLUTE

He is likewise a rival of mine—that is, of my other self's, for he does not think his friend Captain Absolute ever saw the lady in question; and it is ridiculous enough to hear him complain to me of one Beverley, a concealed skulking rival, who——

FAULKLAND

Hush!—he's here.

Enter ACRES

ACRES

Ha! my dear friend, noble captain, and honest Jack, how do'st thou? just arrived, faith, as you see.—Sir, your humble servant. Warm work on the roads,

E   49

Jack!—Odds whips and wheels! I've travelled like a comet, with a tail of dust all the way as long as the Mall.

CAPTAIN ABSOLUTE

Ah! Bob, you are indeed an eccentric planet, but we know your attraction hither.—Give me leave to introduce Mr. Faulkland to you; Mr. Faulkland, Mr. Acres.

ACRES

Sir, I am most heartily glad to see you: sir, I solicit your connections.—Hey, Jack—what, this is Mr. Faulkland, who——

CAPTAIN ABSOLUTE

Ay, Bob, Miss Melville's Mr. Faulkland.

ACRES

Odso! she and your father can be but just arrived before me?—I suppose you have seen them. Ah! Mr. Faulkland, you are indeed a happy man.

FAULKLAND

I have not seen Miss Melville yet, sir;—I hope she enjoyed full health and spirits in Devonshire?

ACRES

Never knew her better in my life, sir,—never better. Odds blushes and blooms! she has been as healthy as the German Spa.

FAULKLAND

Indeed! I did hear that she had been a little indisposed.

ACRES

False, false, sir—only said to vex you: quite the reverse, I assure you.

FAULKLAND

There, Jack, you see she has the advantage of me; I had almost fretted myself ill.

CAPTAIN ABSOLUTE

Now are you angry with your mistress for not having been sick?

FAULKLAND

No, no, you misunderstand me: yet surely a little trifling indisposition is not an unnatural consequence of absence from those we love.—Now confess—isn't there something unkind in this violent, robust, unfeeling health?

CAPTAIN ABSOLUTE

Oh, it was very unkind of her to be well in your absence, to be sure!

ACRES

Good apartments, Jack.

FAULKLAND

Well, sir, but you were saying that Miss Melville has been so exceedingly well—what then she has been merry and gay, I suppose?—Always in spirits—hey?

ACRES

Merry, odds crickets! she has been the belle and spirit of the company wherever she has been—so lively and entertaining! so full of wit and humour!

FAULKLAND

There, Jack, there.—Oh, by my soul! there is an innate levity in woman that nothing can overcome.—What! happy, and I away!

CAPTAIN ABSOLUTE

Have done!—How foolish this is! just now you were only apprehensive for your mistress' spirits.

FAULKLAND

Why, Jack, have I been the joy and spirit of the company?

CAPTAIN ABSOLUTE

No, indeed, you have not.

FAULKLAND

Have I been lively and entertaining?

CAPTAIN ABSOLUTE

Oh, upon my word, I acquit you.

FAULKLAND

Have I been full of wit and humour?

CAPTAIN ABSOLUTE

No, faith, to do you justice, you have been confoundedly stupid indeed.

ACRES

What's the matter with the gentleman?

CAPTAIN ABSOLUTE

He is only expressing his great satisfaction at hearing that Julia has been so well and happy—that's all—hey, Faulkland?

FAULKLAND

Oh! I am rejoiced to hear it—yes, yes, she has a happy disposition!

ACRES

That she has indeed—then she is so accomplished—so sweet a voice—so expert at her harpsichord—such a mistress of flat and sharp, squallante, rumblante, and quiverante!—There was this time month—odds minums and crotchets! how she did chirrup at Mrs. Piano's concert!

FAULKLAND

There again, what say you to this? you see she has been all mirth and song—not a thought of me!

CAPTAIN ABSOLUTE

Pho! man, is not music the food of love?

FAULKLAND

Well, well, it may be so.—Pray, Mr. ——, what's his damned name?—Do you remember what songs Miss Melville sung?

ACRES

Not I indeed.

CAPTAIN ABSOLUTE

Stay, now, they were some pretty melancholy purling-stream airs, I warrant; perhaps you may recollect;—did she sing, *When absent from my soul's delight?*

ACRES

No, that wa'n't it.

CAPTAIN ABSOLUTE

Or, *Go, gentle dales!*   [*Sings.*

ACRES

Oh, no! nothing like it. Odds! now I recollect one of them—*My heart's my own, my will is free.*   [*Sings.*

FAULKLAND

Fool! fool that I am! to fix all my happiness on such a trifler! 'Sdeath! to make herself the pipe and ballad-monger of a circle to soothe her light heart with catches and glees!—What can you say to this, sir?

CAPTAIN ABSOLUTE

Why, that I should be glad to hear my mistress had been so merry, sir.

53

FAULKLAND

Nay, nay, nay—I'm not sorry that she has been happy—no, no, I am glad of that—I would not have had her sad or sick—yet surely a sympathetic heart would have shown itself even in the choice of a song —she might have been temperately healthy, and somehow, plaintively gay;—but she has been dancing too, I doubt not!

ACRES

What does the gentleman say about dancing?

CAPTAIN ABSOLUTE

He says the lady we speak of dances as well as she sings.

ACRES

Ay, truly, does she—there was at our last race ball——

FAULKLAND

Hell and the devil!—There!—there—I told you so! I told you so! Oh! she thrives in my absence!— Dancing! But her whole feelings have been in opposition with mine;—I have been anxious, silent, pensive, sedentary—my days have been hours of care, my nights of watchfulness.—She has been all health! spirit! laugh! song! dance!—Oh! damned, damned levity!

CAPTAIN ABSOLUTE

For heaven's sake, Faulkland, don't expose yourself so!—Suppose she has danced, what then?—does not the ceremony of society often oblige——

FAULKLAND

Well, well, I'll contain myself—perhaps as you say— for form sake.—What, Mr. Acres, you were praising Miss Melville's manner of dancing a minuet—hey?

ACRES

Oh, I dare insure her for that—but what I was going to speak of was her country dancing. Odds swimmings! she has such an air with her!

FAULKLAND

Now disappointment on her!—Defend this, Absolute; why don't you defend this?—Country-dances! jigs and reels! am I to blame now? A minuet I could have forgiven—I should not have minded that—I say I should not have regarded a minuet—but country-dances!—Zounds! had she made one in a cotillon—I believe I could have forgiven even that—but to be monkey-led for a night!—to run the gauntlet through a string of amorous palming puppies!—to show paces like a managed filly!—Oh, Jack, there never can be but one man in the world whom a truly modest and delicate woman ought to pair with in a country-dance; and, even then, the rest of the couples should be her great-uncles and aunts!

CAPTAIN ABSOLUTE

Ay, to be sure!—grandfathers and grandmothers!

FAULKLAND

If there be but one vicious mind in the set, 'twill spread like a contagion—the action of their pulse beats to the lascivious movement of the jig—their quivering, warm-breathed sighs impregnate the very air—the atmosphere becomes electrical to love, and each amorous spark darts through every link of the chain!—I must leave you—I own I am somewhat flurried—and that confounded looby has perceived it.

[*Going.*

55

CAPTAIN ABSOLUTE

Nay, but stay, Faulkland, and thank Mr. Acres for his good news.

FAULKLAND

Damn his news! *[Exit.*

CAPTAIN ABSOLUTE

Ha! ha! ha! poor Faulkland five minutes since— 'nothing on earth could give him a moment's uneasiness!'

ACRES

The gentleman wa'n't angry at my praising his mistress, was he?

CAPTAIN ABSOLUTE

A little jealous, I believe, Bob.

ACRES

You don't say so? Ha! ha! jealous of me—that's a good joke.

CAPTAIN ABSOLUTE

There's nothing strange in that, Bob! let me tell you, that sprightly grace and insinuating manner of yours will do some mischief among the girls here.

ACRES

Ah! you joke—ha! ha! mischief—ha! ha! but you know I am not my own property, my dear Lydia has forestalled me. She could never abide me in the country, because I used to dress so badly—but odds frogs and tambours! I shan't take matters so here, now ancient madam has no voice in it: I'll make my old clothes know who's master. I shall straightway cashier the hunting-frock, and render my leather

ACRES

breeches incapable. My hair has been in training some time.

CAPTAIN ABSOLUTE

Indeed!

ACRES

Ay—and tho'ff the side curls are a little restive, my hind-part takes it very kindly.

CAPTAIN ABSOLUTE

Oh, you'll polish, I doubt not.

ACRES

Absolutely I propose so—then if I can find out this Ensign Beverley, odds triggers and flints! I'll make him know the difference o't.

CAPTAIN ABSOLUTE

Spoke like a man! But pray, Bob, I observe you have got an odd kind of a new method of swearing——

ACRES

Ha! ha! you've taken notice of it—'tis genteel, isn't it!—I didn't invent it myself though; but a commander in our militia, a great scholar, I assure you, says that there is no meaning in the common oaths, and that nothing but their antiquity makes them respectable; because, he says, the ancients would never stick to an oath or two, but would say, by Jove! or by Bacchus! or by Mars! or by Venus! or by Pallas, according to the sentiment: so that to swear with propriety, says my little major, the oath should be an echo to the sense; and this we call the *oath referential*, or *sentimental swearing*—ha! ha! 'tis genteel, isn't it.

CAPTAIN ABSOLUTE

Very genteel, and very new, indeed!—and I dare say will supplant all other figures of imprecation.

ACRES

Ay, ay, the best terms will grow obsolete.—Damns have had their day.

Re-enter FAG

FAG

Sir, there is a gentleman below desires to see you.— Shall I show him into the parlour?

CAPTAIN ABSOLUTE

Ay—you may.

ACRES

Well, I must be gone——

CAPTAIN ABSOLUTE

Stay; who is it, Fag?

FAG

Your father, sir.

CAPTAIN ABSOLUTE

You puppy, why didn't you show him up directly?
                                                    [*Exit* FAG.

ACRES

You have business with Sir Anthony.—I expect a message from Mrs. Malaprop at my lodgings. I have sent also to my dear friend, Sir Lucius O'Trigger. Adieu, Jack! we must meet at night, when you shall give me a dozen bumpers to little Lydia.

CAPTAIN ABSOLUTE

That I will with all my heart.—[*Exit* ACRES.] Now for a parental lecture—I hope he has heard nothing of the business that brought me here—I wish the gout had held him fast in Devonshire, with all my soul!

Enter SIR ANTHONY ABSOLUTE

58

Sir, I am delighted to see you here; looking so well! your sudden arrival at Bath made me apprehensive for your health.

SIR ANTHONY

Very apprehensive, I dare say, Jack.—What, you are recruiting here, hey?

CAPTAIN ABSOLUTE

Yes, sir, I am on duty.

SIR ANTHONY

Well, Jack, I am glad to see you, though I did not expect it, for I was going to write to you on a little matter of business.—Jack, I have been considering that I grow old and infirm, and shall probably not trouble you long.

CAPTAIN ABSOLUTE

Pardon me, sir, I never saw you look more strong and hearty; and I pray frequently that you may continue so.

SIR ANTHONY

I hope your prayers may be heard, with all my heart. Well, then, Jack, I have been considering that I am so strong and hearty I may continue to plague you a long time. Now, Jack, I am sensible that the income of your commission, and what I have hitherto allowed you, is but a small pittance for a lad of your spirit.

CAPTAIN ABSOLUTE

Sir, you are very good.

SIR ANTHONY

And it is my wish, while yet I live, to have my boy make some figure in the world. I have resolved, therefore, to fix you at once in a noble independence.

CAPTAIN ABSOLUTE

Sir, your kindness overpowers me—such generosity makes the gratitude of reason more lively than the sensations even of filial affection.

SIR ANTHONY

I am glad you are so sensible of my attention—and you shall be master of a large estate in a few weeks.

CAPTAIN ABSOLUTE

Let my future life, sir, speak my gratitude; I cannot express the sense I have of your munificence.—Yet, sir, I presume you would not wish me to quit the army?

SIR ANTHONY

Oh, that shall be as your wife chooses.

CAPTAIN ABSOLUTE

My wife, sir!

SIR ANTHONY

Ay, ay, settle that between you—settle that between you.

CAPTAIN ABSOLUTE

A wife, sir, did you say?

SIR ANTHONY

Ay, a wife—why, did not I mention her before?

CAPTAIN ABSOLUTE

Not a word of her, sir.

SIR ANTHONY

Odd so!—I mus'n't forget her though.—Yes, Jack, the independence I was talking of is by marriage—the fortune is saddled with a wife—but I suppose that makes no difference.

CAPTAIN ABSOLUTE

Sir! sir!—you amaze me!

SIR ANTHONY

Why, what the devil's the matter with the fool? Just now you were all gratitude and duty.

CAPTAIN ABSOLUTE

I was, sir—you talked to me of independence and a fortune, but not a word of a wife.

SIR ANTHONY

Why—what difference does that make? Odds life, sir! if you have the estate, you must take it with the live stock on it, as it stands.

CAPTAIN ABSOLUTE

If my happiness is to be the price, I must beg leave to decline the purchase.—Pray, sir, who is the lady?

SIR ANTHONY

What's that to you, sir?—Come, give me your promise to love, and to marry her directly.

CAPTAIN ABSOLUTE

Sure, sir, this is not very reasonable, to summon my affections for a lady I know nothing of!

SIR ANTHONY

I am sure, sir, 'tis more unreasonable in you to object to a lady you know nothing of.

CAPTAIN ABSOLUTE

Then, sir, I must tell you plainly that my inclinations are fixed on another—my heart is engaged to an angel.

SIR ANTHONY

Then pray let it send an excuse. It is very sorry—but business prevents its waiting on her.

CAPTAIN ABSOLUTE

But my vows are pledged to her.

SIR ANTHONY

Let her foreclose, Jack; let her foreclose; they are not worth redeeming; besides, you have the angel's vows in exchange, I suppose; so there can be no loss there.

CAPTAIN ABSOLUTE

You must excuse me, sir, if I tell you, once for all, that in this point I cannot obey you.

SIR ANTHONY

Hark'ee, Jack;—I have heard you for some time with patience—I have been cool—quite cool; but take care —you know I am compliance itself—when I am not thwarted;—no one more easily led—when I have my own way;—but don't put me in a frenzy.

CAPTAIN ABSOLUTE

Sir, I must repeat—in this I cannot obey you.

SIR ANTHONY

Now damn me! if ever I call you Jack again while I live!

CAPTAIN ABSOLUTE

Nay, sir, but hear me.

SIR ANTHONY

Sir, I won't hear a word—not a word! not one word! so give me your promise by a nod—and I'll tell you what, Jack—I mean, you dog—if you don't, by——

CAPTAIN ABSOLUTE

What, sir, promise to link myself to some mass of ugliness! to——

SIR ANTHONY

Zounds! sirrah! the lady shall be as ugly as I choose:
she shall have a hump on each shoulder; she shall be
as crooked as the crescent; her one eye shall roll like
the bull's in Cox's Museum; she shall have a skin like
a mummy, and the beard of a Jew—she shall be all this,
sirrah!—yet I will make you ogle her all day, and sit
up all night to write sonnets on her beauty.

CAPTAIN ABSOLUTE

This is reason and moderation indeed!

SIR ANTHONY

None of your sneering, puppy! no grinning, jackanapes!

CAPTAIN ABSOLUTE

Indeed, sir, I never was in a worse humour for mirth
in my life.

SIR ANTHONY

'Tis false, sir. I know you are laughing in your sleeve;
I know you'll grin when I am gone, sirrah!

CAPTAIN ABSOLUTE

Sir, I hope I know my duty better.

SIR ANTHONY

None of your passion, sir! none of your violence, if
you please!—It won't do with me, I promise you.

CAPTAIN ABSOLUTE

Indeed, sir, I never was cooler in my life.

SIR ANTHONY

'Tis a confounded lie!—I know you are in a passion
in your heart; I know you are, you hypocritical
young dog! but it won't do.

CAPTAIN ABSOLUTE

Nay, sir, upon my word——

SIR ANTHONY

So you will fly out! can't you be cool like me? What
the devil good can passion do?—Passion is of no
service, you impudent, insolent, overbearing repro-
bate!—There, you sneer again! don't provoke me!—
but you rely upon the mildness of my temper—you
do, you dog! you play upon the meekness of my disposition!—Yet take care—the patience of a saint may
be overcome at last!—but mark! I give you six hours
and a half to consider of this: if you then agree, without any condition, to do everything on earth that I
choose, why—confound you! I may in time forgive
you.—If not, zounds! don't enter the same hemi-
sphere with me! don't dare to breathe the same air,
or use the same light with me; but get an atmosphere
and a sun of your own! I'll strip you of your commission; I'll lodge a five-and-threepence in the hands
of trustees, and you shall live on the interest.—I'll
disown you, I'll disinherit you, I'll unget you! and
damn me! if ever I call you Jack again!

[*Exit* SIR ANTHONY.

CAPTAIN ABSOLUTE

Mild, gentle, considerate father—I kiss your hands!
—What a tender method of giving his opinion in
these matters Sir Anthony has! I dare not trust him
with the truth—I wonder what old wealthy hag it is
that he wants to bestow on me!—Yet he married
himself for love! and was in his youth a bold intriguer,
and a gay companion!

Re-enter FAG

FAG

Assuredly, sir, your father is wrath to a degree; he comes down stairs eight or ten steps at a time—muttering, growling, and thumping the banisters all the way: I and the cook's dog stand bowing at the door—rap! he gives me a stroke on the head with his cane; bids me carry that to my master; then kicking the poor turnspit into the area, damns us all, for a puppy triumvirate!—Upon my credit, sir, were I in your place, and found my father such very bad company, I should certainly drop his acquaintance.

CAPTAIN ABSOLUTE

Cease your impertinence, sir, at present.—Did you come in for nothing more?—Stand out of the way!

[*Pushes him aside, and exit.*

FAG

So! Sir Anthony trims my master; he is afraid to reply to his father—then vents his spleen on poor Fag!—When one is vexed by one person, to revenge one's self on another, who happens to come in the way, is the vilest injustice! Ah! it shows the worst temper—the basest——

Enter BOY

BOY

Mr. Fag! Mr. Fag! your master calls you.

FAG

Well, you little dirty puppy, you need not bawl so!—The meanest disposition! the——

BOY

Quick, quick, Mr. Fag!

FAG

Quick! quick! you impudent jackanapes! am I to be commanded by you too? you little, impertinent, insolent, kitchen-bred——

[*Exit kicking and beating him.*

SCENE TWO

The North Parade

Enter LUCY

LUCY

So—I shall have another rival to add to my mistress's list—Captain Absolute. However, I shall not enter his name till my purse has received notice in form. Poor Acres is dismissed!—Well, I have done him a last friendly office, in letting him know that Beverley was here before him.—Sir Lucius is generally more punctual, when he expects to hear from his *dear Dalia*, as he calls her: I wonder he's not here!—I have a little scruple of conscience from this deceit; though I should not be paid so well, if my hero knew that Delia was near fifty, and her own mistress.

Enter SIR LUCIUS O'TRIGGER

SIR LUCIUS

Ha! my little ambassadress—upon my conscience, I have been looking for you; I have been on the South Parade this half hour.

LUCY

[*Speaking simply.*] O gemini! and I have been waiting for your lordship here on the North.

66

SIR LUCIUS

Faith!—may be that was the reason we did not meet; and it is very comical too, how you could go out and I not see you—for I was only taking a nap at the Parade Coffee-house, and I chose the window on purpose that I might not miss you.

LUCY

My stars! Now I'd wager a sixpence I went by while you were asleep.

SIR LUCIUS

Sure enough it must have been so—and I never dreamt it was so late, till I waked. Well, but my little girl, have you got nothing for me?

LUCY

Yes, but I have—I've got a letter for you in my pocket.

SIR LUCIUS

O faith! I guessed you weren't come empty-handed —Well—let me see what the dear creature says.

LUCY

There, Sir Lucius. *[Gives him a letter.*

SIR LUCIUS

[*Reads.*] *Sir—there is often a sudden incentive impulse in love, that has a greater induction than years of domestic combination: such was the commotion I felt at the first superfluous view of Sir Lucius O'Trigger.—* Very pretty, upon my word.—*Female punctuation forbids me to say more; yet let me add, that it will give me joy infallible to find Sir Lucius worthy the last criterion of my affections.* DELIA.

Upon my conscience! Lucy, your lady is a great mistress of language. Faith, she's quite the queen of the dictionary!—for the devil a word dare refuse coming at her call—though one would think it was quite out of hearing.

LUCY

Ay, sir, a lady of her experience——

SIR LUCIUS

Experience! what, at seventeen?

LUCY

O true, sir—but then she reads so—my stars! how she will read off hand!

SIR LUCIUS

Faith, she must be very deep read to write this way—though she is rather an arbitrary writer too—for here are a great many poor words pressed into the service of this note, that would get their *habeas corpus* from any court in Christendom.

LUCY

Ah! Sir Lucius, if you were to hear how she talks of you!

SIR LUCIUS

Oh, tell her I'll make her the best husband in the world, and Lady O'Trigger into the bargain!—But we must get the old gentlewoman's consent—and do everything fairly.

LUCY

Nay, Sir Lucius, I thought you wa'n't rich enough to be so nice.

SIR LUCIUS

Upon my word, young woman, you have hit it:—I

am so poor, that I can't afford to do a dirty action.—
If I did not want money, I'd steal your mistress and
her fortune with a great deal of pleasure.—However,
my pretty girl [*Gives her money*], here's a little something to buy you a ribbon; and meet me in the evening, and I'll give you an answer to this. So, hussy,
take a kiss beforehand to put you in mind.

[*Kisses her*.

LUCY

O Lud! Sir Lucius—I never seed such a gemman!
My lady won't like you if you're so impudent.

SIR LUCIUS

Faith she will, Lucy!—That same—pho! what's the
name of it?—modesty—is a quality in a lover more
praised by the women than liked; so, if your mistress
asks you whether Sir Lucius ever gave you a kiss, tell
her fifty—my dear.

LUCY

What, would you have me tell her a lie?

SIR LUCIUS

Ah, then, you baggage! I'll make it a truth presently.

LUCY

For shame now! here is some one coming.

SIR LUCIUS

Oh, faith, I'll quiet your conscience!

[*Exit humming a tune*.

Enter FAG

FAG

So, so, ma'am! I humbly beg pardon.

LUCY

O Lud! now, Mr. Fag, you flurry one so.

FAG

Come, come, Lucy, here's no one by—so a little less simplicity, with a grain or two more sincerity, if you please.—You play false with us, madam.—I saw you give the baronet a letter.—My master shall know this—and if he don't call him out, I will.

LUCY

Ha! ha! ha! you gentlemen's gentlemen are so hasty. That letter was from Mrs. Malaprop, simpleton.— She is taken with Sir Lucius's address.

FAG

How! what tastes some people have!—Why, I suppose I have walked by her window a hundred times. —But what says our young lady? any message to my master?

LUCY

Sad news, Mr. Fag.—A worse rival than Acres! Sir Anthony Absolute has proposed his son.

FAG

What, Captain Absolute?

LUCY

Even so—I overheard it all.

FAG

Ha! ha! ha! very good, faith. Good bye, Lucy, I must away with this news.

LUCY

Well, you may laugh—but it is true, I assure you.— [*Going.*] But, Mr. Fag, tell your master not to be cast down by this.

FAG

Oh, he'll be so disconsolate!

LUCY

And charge him not to think of quarrelling with young Absolute.

FAG

Never fear! never fear!

LUCY

Be sure—bid him keep up his spirits.

FAG

We will—we will.   [*Exeunt severally.*

ACT THREE

SCENE ONE
The North Parade

Enter CAPTAIN ABSOLUTE

CAPTAIN ABSOLUTE

'Tis just as Fag told me, indeed. Whimsical enough, faith. My father wants to force me to marry the very girl I am plotting to run away with! He must not know of my connection with her yet awhile. He has too summary a method of proceeding in these matters. However, I'll read my recantation instantly. My conversion is something sudden, indeed—but I can assure him it is very sincere. So, so—here he comes. He looks plaguy gruff.   [*Steps aside.*

Enter SIR ANTHONY ABSOLUTE

SIR ANTHONY

No—I'll die sooner than forgive him. Die, did I say? I'll live these fifty years to plague him. At our last meeting, his impudence had almost put me out of temper. An obstinate, passionate, self-willed boy! Who can he take after? This is my return for getting him before all his brothers and sisters!—for putting him, at twelve years old, into a marching regiment, and allowing him fifty pounds a year, besides his pay, ever since! But I have done with him; he's anybody's

· *SIR ANTHONY ABSOLUTE* ·

son for me. I never will see him more, never—never
—never.

CAPTAIN ABSOLUTE
[*Aside, coming forward.*] Now for a penitential face.

SIR ANTHONY
Fellow, get out of my way.

CAPTAIN ABSOLUTE
Sir, you see a penitent before you.

SIR ANTHONY
I see an impudent scoundrel before me.

CAPTAIN ABSOLUTE
A sincere penitent. I am come, sir, to acknowledge my
error, and to submit entirely to your will.

SIR ANTHONY
What's that?

CAPTAIN ABSOLUTE
I have been revolving, and reflecting, and considering on your past goodness, and kindness, and con-
descension to me.

SIR ANTHONY
Well, sir?

CAPTAIN ABSOLUTE
I have been likewise weighing and balancing what
you were pleased to mention concerning duty, and
obedience, and authority.

SIR ANTHONY
Well, puppy?

CAPTAIN ABSOLUTE
Why, then, sir, the result of my reflections is—a

resolution to sacrifice every inclination of my own to your satisfaction.

SIR ANTHONY

Why now you talk sense—absolute sense.—I never heard anything more sensible in my life. Confound you! you shall be Jack again.

CAPTAIN ABSOLUTE

I am happy in the appellation.

SIR ANTHONY

Why, then, Jack, my dear Jack, I will now inform you who the lady really is. Nothing but your passion and violence, you silly fellow, prevented my telling you at first. Prepare, Jack, for wonder and rapture—prepare. What think you of Miss Lydia Languish?

CAPTAIN ABSOLUTE

Languish! What, the Languishes of Worcestershire?

SIR ANTHONY

Worcestershire! no. Did you ever meet Mrs. Malaprop and her niece, Miss Languish, who came into our country just before you were last ordered to your regiment?

CAPTAIN ABSOLUTE

Malaprop! Languish! I don't remember ever to have heard the names before. Yet stay—I think I do recollect something. Languish! Languish! She squints, don't she? A little red-haired girl?

SIR ANTHONY

Squints! A red-haired girl! Zounds! no.

CAPTAIN ABSOLUTE

Then I must have forgot; it can't be the same person.

SIR ANTHONY

Jack! Jack! what think you of blooming, love-breathing seventeen?

CAPTAIN ABSOLUTE

As to that, sir, I am quite indifferent. If I can please you in the matter, 'tis all I desire.

SIR ANTHONY

Nay, but, Jack, such eyes! such eyes! so innocently wild! so bashfully irresolute! not a glance but speaks and kindles some thought of love! Then, Jack, her cheeks! her cheeks, Jack! so deeply blushing, at the insinuations of her tell-tale eyes! Then, Jack, her lips! O, Jack, lips smiling at their own discretion; and if not smiling, more sweetly pouting; more lovely in sullenness.

CAPTAIN ABSOLUTE

That's she, indeed. Well done, old gentleman.

[Aside.

SIR ANTHONY

Then, Jack, her neck! O Jack! Jack!

CAPTAIN ABSOLUTE

And which is to be mine, sir; the niece or the aunt?

SIR ANTHONY

Why, you unfeeling, insensible puppy, I despise you! When I was of your age, such a description would have made me fly like a rocket! The aunt, indeed! Odds life! when I ran away with your mother, I would not have touched anything old or ugly to gain an empire.

CAPTAIN ABSOLUTE

Not to please your father, sir?

75

SIR ANTHONY

To please my father! zounds! not to please—Oh, my father—odd so!—yes—yes; if my father indeed had desired—that's quite another matter. Though he wa'n't the indulgent father that I am, Jack.

CAPTAIN ABSOLUTE

I dare say not, sir.

SIR ANTHONY

But, Jack, you are not sorry to find your mistress is so beautiful?

CAPTAIN ABSOLUTE

Sir, I repeat it—if I please you in this affair, 'tis all I desire. Not that I think a woman the worse for being handsome; but, sir, if you please to recollect, you before hinted something about a hump or two, one eye, and a few more graces of that kind—now, without being very nice, I own I should rather choose a wife of mine to have the usual number of limbs, and a limited quantity of back: and though one eye may be very agreeable, yet as the prejudice has always run in favour of two, I would not wish to affect a singularity in that article.

SIR ANTHONY

What a phlegmatic sot it is! Why, sirrah, you're an anchorite!—a vile, insensible stock. You a soldier!— you're a walking block, fit only to dust the company's regimentals on! Odds life! I have a great mind to marry the girl myself!

CAPTAIN ABSOLUTE

I am entirely at your disposal, sir: if you should think of addressing Miss Languish yourself, I suppose you would have me marry the aunt; or if you should change your mind, and take the old lady—'tis the same to me—I'll marry the niece.

SIR ANTHONY

Upon my word, Jack, thou'rt either a very great hypocrite, or—but, come, I know your indifference on such a subject must be all a lie—I'm sure it must—come, now—damn your demure face!—come, confess, Jack —you have been lying, ha'n't you? You have been playing the hypocrite, hey!—I'll never forgive you, if you ha'n't been lying and playing the hypocrite.

CAPTAIN ABSOLUTE

I'm sorry, sir, that the respect and duty which I bear to you should be so mistaken.

SIR ANTHONY

Hang your respect and duty! But come along with me, I'll write a note to Mrs. Malaprop, and you shall visit the lady directly. Her eyes shall be the Promethean torch to you—come along, I'll never forgive you, if you don't come back stark mad with rapture and impatience—if you don't, egad, I will marry the girl myself! [*Exeunt.*

SCENE TWO

Julia's Dressing-Room

FAULKLAND *discovered alone*

FAULKLAND

They told me Julia would return directly; I wonder she is not yet come! How mean does this captious, unsatisfied temper of mine appear to my cooler judgment! Yet I know not that I indulge it in any other point: but on this one subject, and to this one subject, whom I think I love beyond my life, I am ever ungenerously fretful and madly capricious! I am conscious of it—yet I cannot correct myself! What tender honest joy sparkled in her eyes when we met! how delicate was the warmth of her expression! I was ashamed to appear less happy—though I had come resolved to wear a face of coolness and upbraiding. Sir Anthony's presence prevented my proposed expostulations: yet I must be satisfied that she has not been so very happy in my absence. She is coming! Yes!—I know the nimbleness of her tread, when she thinks her impatient Faulkland counts the moments of her stay.

Enter JULIA

JULIA

I had not hoped to see you again so soon.

FAULKLAND

Could I, Julia, be contented with my first welcome—restrained as we were by the presence of a third person?

JULIA

O Faulkland, when your kindness can make me thus happy, let me not think that I discovered something of coldness in your first salutation.

FAULKLAND

'Twas but your fancy, Julia. I was rejoiced to see you —to see you in such health. Sure I had no cause for coldness?

JULIA

Nay, then, I see you have taken something ill. You must not conceal from me what it is.

FAULKLAND

Well, then—shall I own to you that my joy at hearing of your health and arrival here, by your neighbour Acres, was somewhat damped by his dwelling much on the high spirits you had enjoyed in Devonshire— on your mirth—your singing—dancing, and I know not what! For such is my temper, Julia, that I should regard every mirthful moment in your absence as a treason to constancy. The mutual tear that steals down the cheek of parting lovers is a compact, that no smile shall live there till they meet again.

JULIA

Must I never cease to tax my Faulkland with this teasing minute caprice? Can the idle reports of a silly boor weigh in your breast against my tried affections?

FAULKLAND

They have no weight with me, Julia: No, no—I am happy if you have been so—yet only say, that you did not sing with mirth—say that you thought of Faulk-land in the dance.

JULIA

I never can be happy in your absence. If I wear a countenance of content, it is to show that my mind holds no doubt of my Faulkland's truth. If I seemed sad, it were to make malice triumph; and say, that I fixed my heart on one, who left me to lament his roving, and my own credulity. Believe me, Faulkland, I mean not to upbraid you, when I say, that I have

79

often dressed sorrow in smiles, lest my friends should guess whose unkindness had caused my tears.

FAULKLAND

You were ever all goodness to me. Oh, I am a brute, when I but admit a doubt of your true constancy!

JULIA

If ever without such cause from you, as I will not suppose possible, you find my affections veering but a point, may I become a proverbial scoff for levity and base ingratitude.

FAULKLAND

Ah! Julia, that last word is grating to me. I would I had no title to your gratitude! Search your heart, Julia; perhaps what you have mistaken for love, is but the warm effusion of a too thankful heart.

JULIA

For what quality must I love you?

FAULKLAND

For no quality! To regard me for any quality of mind or understanding, were only to esteem me. And for person—I have often wished myself deformed, to be convinced that I owe no obligation there for any part of your affection.

JULIA

Where nature has bestowed a show of nice attention in the features of a man, he should laugh at it as misplaced. I have seen men, who in this vain article, perhaps, might rank above you; but my heart has never asked my eyes if it were so or not.

FAULKLAND

Now this is not well from you, Julia—I despise

JULIA

person in a man—yet if you loved me as I wish, though I were an Æthiop, you'd think none so fair.

JULIA

I see you are determined to be unkind! The contract which my poor father bound us in gives you more than a lover's privilege.

FAULKLAND

Again, Julia, you raise ideas that feed and justify my doubts. I would not have been more free—no—I am proud of my restraint. Yet—yet—perhaps your high respect alone for this solemn compact has fettered your inclinations, which else had made a worthier choice. How shall I be sure, had you remained un-bound in thought and promise, that I should still have been the object of your persevering love?

JULIA

Then try me now. Let us be free as strangers as to what is past: my heart will not feel more liberty!

FAULKLAND

There now! so hasty, Julia! so anxious to be free! If your love for me were fixed and ardent, you would not lose your hold, even though I wished it!

JULIA

Oh! you torture me to the heart! I cannot bear it.

FAULKLAND

I do not mean to distress you. If I loved you less I should never give you an uneasy moment. But hear me. All my fretful doubts arise from this. Women are not used to weigh and separate the motives of their affections: the cold dictates of prudence, gratitude, or filial duty, may sometimes be mistaken for the pleadings of the heart. I would not boast—yet let me say, that I have neither age, person, nor character, to found dislike on; my fortune such as few ladies could be charged with indiscretion in the match. O Julia! when love receives such countenance from prudence, nice minds will be suspicious of its birth.

JULIA

I know not whither your insinuations would tend: —but as they seem pressing to insult me, I will spare you the regret of having done so.—I have given you no cause for this!   [*Exit in tears.*

FAULKLAND

In tears! Stay, Julia: stay but for a moment.—The door is fastened!—Julia!—my soul—but for one moment!—I hear her sobbing!—'Sdeath! what a brute am I to use her thus! Yet stay! Ay—she is coming now:—how little resolution there is in a woman! —how a few soft words can turn them!—No, faith! —she is not coming either.—Why, Julia—my love— say but that you forgive me—come but to tell me that —now this is being too resentful. Stay! she is coming too—I thought she would—no steadiness in anything: her going away must have been a mere trick then— she sha'n't see that I was hurt by it—I'll affect in-difference—[*Hums a tune; then listens.*] No—zounds! she's not coming!—nor don't intend it, I suppose.— This is not steadiness, but obstinacy! Yet I deserve it.—What, after so long an absence to quarrel with her tenderness!—'twas barbarous and unmanly!—I should be ashamed to see her now.—I'll wait till her just resentment is abated—and when I distress her so again, may I lose her for ever! and be linked instead to some antique virago, whose gnawing passions, and long hoarded spleen, shall make me curse my folly half the day and all the night.　　　　　　　*[Exit.*

SCENE THREE

MRS. MALAPROP's *Lodgings*

MRS. MALAPROP, *with a letter in her hand,*
and CAPTAIN ABSOLUTE

MRS. MALAPROP
Your being Sir Anthony's son, captain, would itself be a sufficient accommodation; but from the ingenuity of your appearance, I am convinced you deserve the character here given of you.

CAPTAIN ABSOLUTE
Permit me to say, madam, that as I never yet have had the pleasure of seeing Miss Languish, my principal inducement in this affair at present is the honour of being allied to Mrs. Malaprop; of whose intellectual accomplishments, elegant manners, and unaffected learning, no tongue is silent.

MRS. MALAPROP
Sir, you do me infinite honour! I beg, captain, you'll be seated.—[*They sit.*] Ah! few gentlemen, now-a-days, know how to value the ineffectual qualities in a woman!—few think how a little knowledge becomes a gentlewoman.—Men have no sense now but for the worthless flower of beauty!

CAPTAIN ABSOLUTE
It is but too true, indeed, ma'am;—yet I fear our ladies should share the blame—they think our

admiration of beauty so great, that knowledge in them would be superfluous. Thus, like garden-trees, they seldom show fruit, till time has robbed them of more specious blossom.—Few, like Mrs. Malaprop and the orange-tree, are rich in both at once!

MRS. MALAPROP

Sir, you overpower me with good-breeding.—He is the very pine-apple of politeness!—You are not ignorant, captain, that this giddy girl has somehow contrived to fix her affections on a beggarly, strolling, eavesdropping ensign, whom none of us have seen, and nobody knows anything of.

CAPTAIN ABSOLUTE

Oh, I have heard the silly affair before.—I'm not at all prejudiced against her on that account.

MRS. MALAPROP

You are very good and very considerate, captain. I am sure I have done everything in my power since I exploded the affair; long ago I laid my positive conjunctions on her, never to think on the fellow again; —I have since laid Sir Anthony's preposition before her; but, I am sorry to say, she seems resolved to decline every particle that I enjoin her.

CAPTAIN ABSOLUTE

It must be very distressing, indeed, ma'am.

MRS. MALAPROP

Oh! it gives me the hydrostatics to such a degree.—I thought she had persisted from corresponding with him; but, behold, this very day, I have interceded another letter from the fellow; I believe I have it in my pocket.

CAPTAIN ABSOLUTE
Oh, the devil! my last note.   [*Aside.*

MRS. MALAPROP
Ay, here it is.

CAPTAIN ABSOLUTE
Ay, my note indeed! Oh, the little traitress Lucy.
[*Aside.*

MRS. MALAPROP
There, perhaps you may know the writing.
[*Gives him the letter.*

CAPTAIN ABSOLUTE
I think I have seen the hand before—yes, I certainly
must have seen this hand before——

MRS. MALAPROP
Nay, but read it, captain.

CAPTAIN ABSOLUTE
[*Reads.*] *My soul's idol, my adored Lydia!*—Very
tender, indeed!

MRS. MALAPROP
Tender, ay, and profane too, o' my conscience.

CAPTAIN ABSOLUTE
[*Reads.*] *I am excessively alarmed at the intelligence you
send me, the more so as my new rival*——

MRS. MALAPROP
That's you, sir.

CAPTAIN ABSOLUTE
[*Reads.*] *Has universally the character of being an
accomplished gentleman and a man of honour.*—Well,
that's handsome enough.

MRS. MALAPROP
Oh, the fellow has some design in writing so.

85

CAPTAIN ABSOLUTE

That he had, I'll answer for him, ma'am.

MRS. MALAPROP

But go on, sir—you'll see presently.

CAPTAIN ABSOLUTE

[*Reads.*] *As for the old weather-beaten she-dragon who guards you*—Who can he mean by that?

MRS. MALAPROP

Me, sir!—me!—he means me!—There—what do you think now?—but go on a little further.

CAPTAIN ABSOLUTE

Impudent scoundrel!—[*Reads.*] *it shall go hard but I will elude her vigilance, as I am told that the same ridiculous vanity, which makes her dress up her coarse features, and deck her dull chat with hard words which she don't understand——*

MRS. MALAPROP

There, sir, an attack upon my language! what do you think of that?—an aspersion upon my parts of speech! was ever such a brute! Sure, if I reprehend any thing in this world it is the use of my oracular tongue, and a nice derangement of epitaphs!

CAPTAIN ABSOLUTE

He deserves to be hanged and quartered! let me see— [*Reads.*] *same ridiculous vanity——*

MRS. MALAPROP

You need not read it again, sir.

CAPTAIN ABSOLUTE

I beg pardon, ma'am.—[*Reads.*] *does also lay her open to the grossest deceptions from flattery and pretended*

86

admiration—an impudent coxcomb!—*so that I have a scheme to see you shortly with the old harridan's consent, and even to make her a go-between in our interview.*—Was ever such assurance!

MRS. MALAPROP

Did you ever hear anything like it?—he'll elude my vigilance, will he?—Yes, yes! ha! ha! he's very likely to enter these doors;—we'll try who can plot best!

CAPTAIN ABSOLUTE

So we will, ma'am—so we will! Ha! ha! ha! a conceited puppy, ha! ha! ha!—Well, but, Mrs. Malaprop, as the girl seems so infatuated by this fellow, suppose you were to wink at her corresponding with him for a little time—let her even plot an elopement with him —then do you connive at her escape—while I, just in the nick, will have the fellow laid by the heels, and fairly contrive to carry her off in his stead.

MRS. MALAPROP

I am delighted with the scheme; never was anything better perpetrated!

CAPTAIN ABSOLUTE

But, pray, could not I see the lady for a few minutes now?—I should like to try her temper a little.

MRS. MALAPROP

Why, I don't know—I doubt she is not prepared for a visit of this kind. There is a decorum in these matters.

CAPTAIN ABSOLUTE

O Lord! she won't mind me—only tell her Beverley——

MRS. MALAPROP

Sir!

CAPTAIN ABSOLUTE
Gently, good tongue.   [*Aside.*

MRS. MALAPROP
What did you say of Beverley?

CAPTAIN ABSOLUTE
Oh, I was going to propose that you should tell her, by way of jest, that it was Beverley who was below; she'd come down fast enough then—ha! ha! ha!

MRS. MALAPROP
'Twould be a trick she well deserves; besides, you know the fellow tells her he'll get my consent to see her—ha! ha! Let him if he can, I say again. Lydia, come down here!—[*Calling.*] He'll make me a go-between in their interviews!—ha! ha! ha! Come down, I say, Lydia! I don't wonder at your laughing, ha! ha! ha! his impudence is truly ridiculous.

CAPTAIN ABSOLUTE
'Tis very ridiculous, upon my soul, ma'am, ha! ha! ha!

MRS. MALAPROP
The little hussy won't hear. Well, I'll go and tell her at once who it is—she shall know that Captain Absolute is come to wait on her. And I'll make her behave as becomes a young woman.

CAPTAIN ABSOLUTE
As you please, madam.

MRS. MALAPROP
For the present, captain, your servant. Ah! you've not done laughing yet, I see—elude my vigilance; yes, yes; ha! ha! ha!   [*Exit.*

CAPTAIN ABSOLUTE

Ha! ha! ha! one would think now that I might throw off all disguise at once, and seize my prize with security; but such is Lydia's caprice, that to undeceive were probably to lose her. I'll see whether she knows me.

[Walks aside, and seems engaged in looking at the pictures.

Enter LYDIA

LYDIA

What a scene am I now to go through! surely nothing can be more dreadful than to be obliged to listen to the loathsome addresses of a stranger to one's heart. I have heard of girls persecuted as I am, who have appealed in behalf of their favoured lover to the generosity of his rival; suppose I were to try it—there stands the hated rival—an officer too;—but oh, how unlike my Beverley! I wonder he don't begin—truly he seems a very negligent wooer!—quite at his ease, upon my word! I'll speak first—Mr. Absolute.

CAPTAIN ABSOLUTE

Ma'am.   *[Turns round.*

LYDIA

O heavens! Beverley!

CAPTAIN ABSOLUTE

Hush;—hush, my life! softly! be not surprised!

LYDIA

I am so astonished! and so terrified! and so overjoyed!—for Heaven's sake! how came you here?

CAPTAIN ABSOLUTE

Briefly, I have deceived your aunt—I was informed

that my new rival was to visit here this evening, and contriving to have him kept away, have passed myself on her for Captain Absolute.

LYDIA

O charming! And she really takes you for young Absolute.

CAPTAIN ABSOLUTE

Oh, she's convinced of it.

LYDIA

Ha! ha! ha! I can't forbear laughing to think how her sagacity is overreached!

CAPTAIN ABSOLUTE

But we trifle with our precious moments—such another opportunity may not occur; then let me conjure my kind, my condescending angel, to fix the time when I may rescue her from undeserving persecution, and with a licensed warmth plead for my reward.

LYDIA

Will you then, Beverley, consent to forfeit that portion of my paltry wealth?—that burden on the wings of love?

CAPTAIN ABSOLUTE

Oh, come to me—rich only thus—in loveliness! Bring no portion to me but thy love—'twill be generous in you, Lydia,—for well you know it is the only dower your poor Beverley can repay.

LYDIA

How persuasive are his words!—how charming will poverty be with him!   [*Aside*.

CAPTAIN ABSOLUTE

Ah! my soul, what a life will we then live! Love shall be our idol and support! we will worship him with a monastic strictness; abjuring all worldly toys, to centre every thought and action there. Proud of calamity, we will enjoy the wreck of wealth; while the surrounding gloom of adversity shall make the flame of our pure love show doubly bright. By Heavens! I would fling all goods of fortune from me with a prodigal hand, to enjoy the scene where I might clasp my Lydia to my bosom, and say, the world affords no smile to me but here—[*Embracing her.*] If she holds out now, the devil is in it! [*Aside.*

LYDIA

Now could I fly with him to the antipodes! but my persecution is not yet come to a crisis. [*Aside.*

Re-enter MRS. MALAPROP, *listening*

MRS. MALAPROP

I am impatient to know how the little hussy deports herself. [*Aside.*

CAPTAIN ABSOLUTE

So pensive, Lydia!—is then your warmth abated?

MRS. MALAPROP

Warmth abated!—so!—she has been in a passion, I suppose. [*Aside.*

LYDIA

No—nor ever can while I have life.

MRS. MALAPROP

An ill-tempered little devil! She'll be in a passion all her life—will she? [*Aside.*

LYDIA

Think not the idle threats of my ridiculous aunt can ever have any weight with me.

MRS. MALAPROP

Very dutiful, upon my word!   [*Aside.*

LYDIA

Let her choice be Captain Absolute, but Beverley is mine.

MRS. MALAPROP

I am astonished at her assurance!—to his face—this is to his face.   [*Aside.*

CAPTAIN ABSOLUTE

Thus then let me enforce my suit.   [*Kneeling.*

MRS. MALAPROP

[*Aside.*] Ay, poor young man!—down on his knees entreating for pity!—I can contain no longer.—[*Coming forward.*] Why, thou vixen!—I have overheard you.

CAPTAIN ABSOLUTE

Oh, confound her vigilance!   [*Aside.*

MRS. MALAPROP

Captain Absolute, I know not how to apologize for her shocking rudeness.

CAPTAIN ABSOLUTE

[*Aside.*] So all's safe, I find.—[*Aloud.*] I have hopes, madam, that time will bring the young lady——

MRS. MALAPROP

Oh, there's nothing to be hoped for from her! she's as headstrong as an allegory on the banks of Nile.

LYDIA

Nay, madam, what do you charge me with now?

MRS. MALAPROP

Why, thou unblushing rebel—didn't you tell this gentleman to his face that you loved another better? —didn't you say you never would be his?

LYDIA

No, madam—I did not.

MRS. MALAPROP

Good heavens! what assurance!—Lydia, Lydia, you ought to know that lying don't become a young woman!—Didn't you boast that Beverley, that stroller Beverley, possessed your heart?—Tell me that, I say.

LYDIA

'Tis true, ma'am, and none but Beverley——

MRS. MALAPROP

Hold!—hold, Assurance!—you shall not be so rude.

CAPTAIN ABSOLUTE

Nay, pray, Mrs. Malaprop, don't stop the young lady's speech: she's very welcome to talk thus—it does not hurt me in the least, I assure you.

MRS. MALAPROP

You are too good, captain—too amiably patient—but come with me, miss.—Let us see you again soon, captain—remember what we have fixed.

CAPTAIN ABSOLUTE

I shall, ma'am.

MRS. MALAPROP

Come, take a graceful leave of the gentleman.

LYDIA

May every blessing wait on my Beverley, my loved Bev——

MRS. MALAPROP

Hussy! I'll choke the word in your throat!—come along—come along.

> [*Exeunt severally;* CAPTAIN ABSOLUTE *kissing his hand to* LYDIA—MRS. MALA-PROP *stopping her from speaking.*

SCENE FOUR

ACRES' *Lodgings*

ACRES, *as just dressed, and* DAVID

ACRES

Indeed, David—do you think I become it so?

DAVID

You are quite another creature, believe me, master, by the mass! an' we've any luck we shall see the Devon monkeyrony in all the print-shops in Bath!

ACRES

Dress does make a difference, David.

DAVID

'Tis all in all, I think.—Difference! why, an' you were to go now to Clod Hall, I am certain the old lady wouldn't know you: Master Butler wouldn't believe his own eyes, and Mrs. Pickle would cry, Lard preserve me! our dairy-maid would come giggling to the door, and I warrant Dolly Tester, your honour's favourite, would blush like my waistcoat.—Oons! I'll hold a gallon, there an't a dog in the house but would bark, and I question whether Phillis would wag a hair of her tail!

94

ACRES

Ay, David, there's nothing like polishing.

DAVID

So I says of your honour's boots; but the boy never heeds me!

ACRES

But, David, has Mr. De-la-grace been here? I must rub up my balancing, and chasing, and boring.

DAVID

I'll call again, sir.

ACRES

Do—and see if there are any letters for me at the post-office.

DAVID

I will.—By the mass, I can't help looking at your head!—if I hadn't been by at the cooking, I wish I may die if I should have known the dish again myself.

[*Exit.*

ACRES

[*Practising a dancing-step.*] Sink, slide—coupee.— Confound the first inventors of cotillons! say I—they are as bad as algebra to us country gentlemen.—I can walk a minuet easy enough when I am forced!—and I have been accounted a good stick in a country-dance.—Odds jigs and tabors! I never valued your cross-over to couple—figure in—right and left—and I'd foot it with e'er a captain in the county!—but these outlandish heathen allemandes and cotillons are quite beyond me!—I shall never prosper at 'em, that's sure—mine are true-born English legs—they don't understand their curst French lingo!—their *pas* this,

95

and *pas* that, and *pas* t'other!—damn me!—my feet
don't like to be called paws! no, 'tis certain I have
most Anti-gallican toes!

Enter SERVANT

SERVANT
Here is Sir Lucius O'Trigger to wait on you, sir.

ACRES
Show him in.   [*Exit* SERVANT.

Enter SIR LUCIUS O'TRIGGER

SIR LUCIUS
Mr. Acres, I am delighted to embrace you.

ACRES
My dear Sir Lucius, I kiss your hands.

SIR LUCIUS
Pray, my friend, what has brought you so suddenly
to Bath?

ACRES
Faith! I have followed Cupid's Jack-a-lantern, and find
myself in a quagmire at last.—In short, I have been
very ill-used, Sir Lucius.—I don't choose to mention
names, but look on me as on a very ill-used gentleman.

SIR LUCIUS
Pray what is the case?—I ask no names.

ACRES
Mark me, Sir Lucius, I fall as deep as need be in love
with a young lady—her friends take my part—I
follow her to Bath—send word of my arrival; and
receive answer, that the lady is to be otherwise dis-
posed of.—This, Sir Lucius, I call being ill-used.

SIR LUCIUS O'TRIGGER

SIR LUCIUS

Very ill, upon my conscience.—Pray, can you divine the cause of it?

ACRES

Why, there's the matter; she has another lover, one Beverley, who, I am told, is now in Bath.—Odds slanders and lies! he must be at the bottom of it.

SIR LUCIUS

A rival in the case, is there?—and you think he has supplanted you unfairly?

ACRES

Unfairly! to be sure he has. He never could have done it fairly.

SIR LUCIUS

Then sure you know what is to be done!

ACRES

Not I, upon my soul!

SIR LUCIUS

We wear no swords here, but you understand me.

ACRES

What! fight him.

SIR LUCIUS

Ay, to be sure: what can I mean else?

ACRES

But he has given me no provocation.

SIR LUCIUS

Now, I think he has given you the greatest provocation in the world. Can a man commit a more heinous offence against another man than to fall in love with the same woman? Oh, by my soul! it is the most unpardonable breach of friendship.

I   97

ACRES

Breach of friendship! ay, ay; but I have no acquaintance with this man. I never saw him in my life.

SIR LUCIUS

That's no argument at all—he has the less right then to take such a liberty.

ACRES

Gad, that's true—I grow full of anger, Sir Lucius!—I fire apace! Odds hilts and blades! I find a man may have a deal of valour in him, and not know it! But couldn't I contrive to have a little right on my side?

SIR LUCIUS

What the devil signifies right, when your honour is concerned? Do you think Achilles, or my little Alexander the Great, ever inquired where the right lay? No, by my soul, they drew their broad-swords, and left the lazy sons of peace to settle the justice of it.

ACRES

Your words are a grenadier's march to my heart! I believe courage must be catching! I certainly do feel a kind of valour rising as it were—a kind of courage, as I may say.—Odds flints, pans, and triggers! I'll challenge him directly.

SIR LUCIUS

Ah, my little friend, if I had Blunderbuss Hall here, I could show you a range of ancestry, in the old O'Trigger line, that would furnish the new room; every one of whom had killed his man!—For though the mansion-house and dirty acres have slipped through my fingers, I thank heaven our honour and the family-pictures are as fresh as ever.

ACRES

O, Sir Lucius! I have had ancestors too!—every man of 'em colonel or captain in the militia!—Odds balls and barrels! say no more—I'm braced for it. The thunder of your words has soured the milk of human kindness in my breast:—Zounds! as the man in the plays says, *I could do such deeds!*

SIR LUCIUS

Come, come, there must be no passion at all in the case—these things should always be done civilly.

ACRES

I must be in a passion, Sir Lucius—I must be in a rage.—Dear Sir Lucius, let me be in a rage, if you love me. Come, here's pen and paper.—[*Sits down to write.*] I would the ink were red!—Indite, I say, indite!—How shall I begin? Odds bullets and blades! I'll write a good bold hand, however.

SIR LUCIUS

Pray compose yourself.

ACRES

Come—now, shall I begin with an oath? Do, Sir Lucius, let me begin with a damme.

SIR LUCIUS

Pho! pho! do the thing decently, and like a Christian. Begin now—Sir——

ACRES

That's too civil by half.

SIR LUCIUS

To prevent the confusion that might arise——

ACRES

Well—

99

SIR LUCIUS

From our both addressing the same lady——

ACRES

Ay, there's the reason—*same lady*—well——

SIR LUCIUS

I shall expect the honour of your company——

ACRES

Zounds! I'm not asking him to dinner.

SIR LUCIUS

Pray be easy.

ACRES

Well, then, *honour of your company*——

SIR LUCIUS

To settle our pretensions——

ACRES

Well.

SIR LUCIUS

Let me see, ay, King's-Mead-Fields will do—*in King's-Mead-Fields.*

ACRES

So, that's done—Well, I'll fold it up presently; my own crest—a hand and dagger shall be the seal.

SIR LUCIUS

You see now this little explanation will put a stop at once to all confusion or misunderstanding that might arise between you.

ACRES

Ay, we fight to prevent any misunderstanding.

SIR LUCIUS

Now, I'll leave you to fix your own time.—Take my

advice, and you'll decide it this evening if you can; then let the worst come of it, 'twill be off your mind to-morrow.

ACRES

Very true.

SIR LUCIUS

So I shall see nothing of you, unless it be by letter, till the evening.—I would do myself the honour to carry your message; but, to tell you a secret, I believe I shall have just such another affair on my own hands. There is a gay captain here, who put a jest on me lately, at the expense of my country, and I only want to fall in with the gentleman, to call him out.

ACRES

By my valour, I should like to see you fight first! Odds life! I should like to see you kill him, if it was only to get a little lesson.

SIR LUCIUS

I shall be very proud of instructing you. Well for the present—but remember now, when you meet your antagonist, do every thing in a mild and agreeable manner.—Let your courage be as keen, but at the same time as polished, as your sword.

[*Exeunt severally.*

ACT FOUR

SCENE ONE

ACRES' *Lodgings*

ACRES *and* DAVID

DAVID

Then, by the mass, sir! I would do no such thing—
ne'er a St. Lucius O'Trigger in the kingdom should
make me fight, when I wasn't so minded. Oons! what
will the old lady say, when she hears o't?

ACRES

Ah! David, if you had heard Sir Lucius!—Odds
sparks and flames! he would have roused your valour.

DAVID

Not he, indeed. I hates such bloodthirsty cormorants.
Look'ee, master, if you wanted a bout at boxing,
quarter-staff, or short-staff, I should never be the man
to bid you cry off: but for your curst sharps and
snaps, I never knew any good come of 'em.

ACRES

But my honour, David, my honour! I must be very
careful of my honour.

DAVID

Ay, by the mass! and I would be very careful of it;
and I think in return my honour couldn't do less than
to be very careful of me.

ACRES

Odds blades! David, no gentleman will ever risk the loss of his honour!

DAVID

I say then, it would be but civil in honour never to risk the loss of a gentleman.—Look'ee, master, this honour seems to me to be a marvellous false friend: ay, truly, a very courtier-like servant.—Put the case, I was a gentleman (which, thank God, no one can say of me); well—my honour makes me quarrel with another gentleman of my acquaintance.—So—we fight. (Pleasant enough that!) Boh;—I kill him—(the more's my luck!) now, pray who gets the profit of it? —Why, my honour. But put the case that he kills me!—by the mass! I go to the worms, and my honour whips over to my enemy.

ACRES

No, David—in that case!—odds crowns and laurels! your honour follows you to the grave.

DAVID

Now, that's just the place where I could make a shift to do without it.

ACRES

Zounds! David, you are a coward!—It doesn't become my valour to listen to you.—What, shall I disgrace my ancestors?—Think of that, David—think what it would be to disgrace my ancestors!

DAVID

Under favour, the surest way of not disgracing them, is to keep as long as you can out of their company. Look'ee now, master, to go to them in such haste—

with an ounce of lead in your brains—I should think might as well be let alone. Our ancestors are very good kind of folks; but they are the last people I should choose to have a visiting acquaintance with.

ACRES

But, David, now, you don't think there is such very, very, very great danger, hey?—Odds life! people often fight without any mischief done!

DAVID

By the mass, I think 'tis ten to one against you!—Oons! here to meet some lion-hearted fellow, I warrant, with his damned double-barrelled swords, and cut-and-thrust pistols! Lord bless us! it makes me tremble to think o't—Those be such desperate bloody-minded weapons! Well, I never could abide 'em!—from a child I never could fancy 'em!—I suppose there an't been so merciless a beast in the world as your loaded pistol!

ACRES

Zounds! I won't be afraid!—Odds fire and fury! you shan't make me afraid—Here is the challenge, and I have sent for my dear friend Jack Absolute to carry it for me.

DAVID

Ay, i' the name of mischief, let him be the messenger. —For my part I wouldn't lend a hand to it for the best horse in your stable. By the mass! it don't look like another letter! It is, as I may say, a designing and malicious-looking letter; and I warrant smells of gunpowder like a soldier's pouch!—Oons! I wouldn't swear it mayn't go off!

DAVID

ACRES

Out, you poltroon! you han't the valour of a grass-hopper.

DAVID

Well, I say no more—'twill be sad news, to be sure, at Clod Hall! but I ha' done. How Phillis will howl when she hears of it!—Ah, poor bitch, she little thinks what shooting her master's going after! And I warrant old Crop, who has carried your honour, field and road, these ten years, will curse the hour he was born.
                                                        [*Whimpering.*

ACRES

It won't do, David—I am determined to fight—so get along, you coward, while I'm in the mind.

Enter SERVANT

SERVANT

Captain Absolute, sir.

ACRES

Oh! show him up.   [*Exit* SERVANT.

DAVID

Well, Heaven send we be all alive this time tomorrow.

ACRES

What's that?—Don't provoke me, David!

DAVID

Good-bye, master.   [*Whimpering.*

ACRES

Get along, you cowardly, dastardly, croaking raven!
                                                        [*Exit* DAVID.

Enter CAPTAIN ABSOLUTE

CAPTAIN ABSOLUTE

What's the matter, Bob?

K   105

ACRES

A vile, sheep-hearted blockhead! If I hadn't the valour of St. George and the dragon to boot——

CAPTAIN ABSOLUTE

But what did you want with me, Bob?

ACRES

Oh!—There——   [*Gives him the challenge.*

CAPTAIN ABSOLUTE

[*Aside.*] *To Ensign Beverley.*—So, what's going on now?—[*Aloud.*] Well, what's this?

ACRES

A challenge!

CAPTAIN ABSOLUTE

Indeed! Why, you won't fight him; will you, Bob?

ACRES

Egad, but I will, Jack. Sir Lucius has wrought me to it. He has left me full of rage—and I'll fight this evening, that so much good passion mayn't be wasted.

CAPTAIN ABSOLUTE

But what have I to do with this?

ACRES

Why, as I think you know something of this fellow, I want you to find him out for me, and give him this mortal defiance.

CAPTAIN ABSOLUTE

Well, give it to me, and trust me he gets it.

ACRES

Thank you, my dear friend, my dear Jack; but it is giving you a great deal of trouble.

106

CAPTAIN ABSOLUTE

Not in the least—I beg you won't mention it.—No trouble in the world, I assure you.

ACRES

You are very kind.—What it is to have a friend!— You couldn't be my second, could you, Jack?

CAPTAIN ABSOLUTE

Why no, Bob—not in this affair—it would not be quite so proper.

ACRES

Well, then, I must get my friend Sir Lucius. I shall have your good wishes, however, Jack?

CAPTAIN ABSOLUTE

Whenever he meets you, believe me.

Re-enter SERVANT

SERVANT

Sir Anthony Absolute is below, inquiring for the captain.

CAPTAIN ABSOLUTE

I'll come instantly.—[*Exit* SERVANT.] Well, my little hero, success attend you.   [*Going.*

ACRES

Stay—stay, Jack.—If Beverley should ask you what kind of a man your friend Acres is, do tell him I am a devil of a fellow—will you, Jack?

CAPTAIN ABSOLUTE

To be sure I shall. I'll say you are a determined dog— hey, Bob?

ACRES

Ah, do, do—and if that frightens him, egad, perhaps

he mayn't come. So tell him I generally kill a man a week; will you, Jack?

CAPTAIN ABSOLUTE

I will, I will; I'll say you are called in the country Fighting Bob.

ACRES

Right—right—'tis all to prevent mischief; for I don't want to take his life if I clear my honour.

CAPTAIN ABSOLUTE

No!—that's very kind of you.

ACRES

Why, you don't wish me to kill him—do you, Jack?

CAPTAIN ABSOLUTE

No, upon my soul, I do not. But a devil of a fellow, hey? [*Going.*

ACRES

True, true—but stay—stay, Jack,—you may add, that you never saw me in such a rage before—a most devouring rage!

CAPTAIN ABSOLUTE

I will, I will.

ACRES

Remember, Jack—a determined dog!

CAPTAIN ABSOLUTE

Ay, ay, Fighting Bob! [*Exeunt severally.*

SCENE TWO

MRS. MALAPROP'S *Lodgings*

MRS. MALAPROP *and* LYDIA

MRS. MALAPROP

Why, thou perverse one!—tell me what you can object to him? Isn't he a handsome man?—tell me that. A genteel man? a pretty figure of a man?

LYDIA

[*Aside.*] She little thinks whom she is praising!—[*Aloud.*] So is Beverley, ma'am.

MRS. MALAPROP

No caparisons, miss, if you please. Caparisons don't become a young woman. No! Captain Absolute is indeed a fine gentleman!

LYDIA

Ay, the Captain Absolute you have seen.   [*Aside.*

MRS. MALAPROP

Then he's so well bred;—so full of alacrity, and adulation!—and has so much to say for himself:—in such good language, too! His physiognomy so grammatical! Then his presence is so noble! I protest, when I saw him, I thought of what Hamlet says in the play:—

'Hesperian curls—the front of Job himself!—
An eye, like March, to threaten at command!—
A station, like Harry Mercury, new—'

Something about kissing—on a hill—however, the similitude struck me directly.

LYDIA

How enraged she'll be presently, when she discovers
her mistake!   [*Aside.*

Enter SERVANT

SERVANT

Sir Anthony and Captain Absolute are below, ma'am.

MRS. MALAPROP

Show them up here.—[*Exit* SERVANT.] Now, Lydia,
I insist on your behaving as becomes a young woman.
Show your good breeding, at least, though you have
forgot your duty.

LYDIA

Madam, I have told you my resolution!—I shall not
only give him no encouragement, but I won't even
speak to, or look at him.

   [*Flings herself into a chair, with her face from the door.*

Enter SIR ANTHONY ABSOLUTE *and*
CAPTAIN ABSOLUTE

SIR ANTHONY

Here we are, Mrs. Malaprop; come to mitigate the
frowns of unrelenting beauty,—and difficulty enough
I had to bring this fellow.—I don't know what's the
matter; but if I had not held him by force, he'd have
given me the slip.

MRS. MALAPROP

You have infinite trouble, Sir Anthony, in the affair.
I am ashamed for the cause!—[*Aside to* LYDIA.]
Lydia, Lydia, rise, I beseech you!—pay your respects!

SIR ANTHONY

I hope, madam, that Miss Languish has reflected on

the worth of this gentleman, and the regard due to her aunt's choice, and my alliance.—[*Aside to* CAPTAIN ABSOLUTE.] Now, Jack, speak to her.

CAPTAIN ABSOLUTE

[*Aside.*] What the devil shall I do!—[*Aside to* SIR ANTHONY.] You see, sir, she won't even look at me whilst you are here. I knew she wouldn't! I told you so. Let me entreat you, sir, to leave us together!
                              [*Seems to expostulate with his father.*

LYDIA

[*Aside.*] I wonder I han't heard my aunt exclaim yet! sure she can't have looked at him!—perhaps the regimentals are alike, and she is something blind.

SIR ANTHONY

I say, sir, I won't stir a foot yet!

MRS. MALAPROP

I am sorry to say, Sir Anthony, that my affluence over my niece is very small.—[*Aside to* LYDIA.] Turn round, Lydia: I blush for you!

SIR ANTHONY

May I not flatter myself, that Miss Languish will assign what cause of dislike she can have to my son! —[*Aside to* CAPTAIN ABSOLUTE.] Why don't you begin, Jack?—Speak, you puppy—speak!

MRS. MALAPROP

It is impossible, Sir Anthony, she can have any. She will not say she has.—[*Aside to* LYDIA.] Answer, hussy! why don't you answer?

SIR ANTHONY

Then, madam, I trust that a childish and hasty predilection will be no bar to Jack's happiness.—[*Aside to* CAPTAIN ABSOLUTE.] Zounds! sirrah! why don't you speak?

LYDIA

[*Aside.*] I think my lover seems as little inclined to conversation as myself.—How strangely blind my aunt must be!

CAPTAIN ABSOLUTE

Hem! hem! madam—hem!—[*Attempts to speak, then returns to* SIR ANTHONY.] Faith! sir, I am so confounded!—and—so—so—confused!—I told you I should be so, sir—I knew it.—The—the—tremor of my passion entirely takes away my presence of mind.

SIR ANTHONY

But it don't take away your voice, fool, does it?—Go up, and speak to her directly!

> [CAPTAIN ABSOLUTE *makes signs to* MRS. MALAPROP *to leave them together.*

MRS. MALAPROP

Sir Anthony, shall we leave them together?—[*Aside to* LYDIA.] Ah! you stubborn little vixen!

SIR ANTHONY

Not yet, ma'am, not yet!—[*Aside to* CAPTAIN ABSOLUTE.] What the devil are you at? unlock your jaws, sirrah, or——

CAPTAIN ABSOLUTE

[*Aside.*] Now Heaven send she may be too sullen to look round!—I must disguise my voice.—[*Draws near* LYDIA, *and speaks in a low hoarse tone.*] Will not Miss Languish lend an ear to the mild accents of true love? Will not——

SIR ANTHONY

What the devil ails the fellow? why don't you speak out?—not stand croaking like a frog in a quinsy!

CAPTAIN ABSOLUTE

The—the—excess of my awe, and my—my—modesty quite choke me!

SIR ANTHONY

Ah! your modesty again!—I'll tell you what, Jack, if you don't speak out directly, and glibly too, I shall be in such a rage!—Mrs. Malaprop, I wish the lady would favour us with something more than a side-front.   [MRS. MALAPROP *seems to chide* LYDIA.

CAPTAIN ABSOLUTE

[*Aside.*] So all will out, I see!—[*Goes up to* LYDIA, *speaks softly.*] Be not surprised, my Lydia, suppress all surprise at present.

LYDIA

[*Aside.*] Heavens! 'tis Beverley's voice! Sure he can't have imposed on Sir Anthony too!—[*Looks round by degrees, then starts up.*] Is this possible?—my Beverley! —how can this be?—my Beverley?

CAPTAIN ABSOLUTE

Ah! 'tis all over.   [*Aside.*

SIR ANTHONY

Beverley!—the devil—Beverley!—What can the girl mean?—this is my son, Jack Absolute.

MRS. MALAPROP

For shame, hussy! for shame! your head runs so on that fellow, that you have him always in your eyes!— beg Captain Absolute's pardon directly.

LYDIA

I see no Captain Absolute, but my loved Beverley!

SIR ANTHONY

Zounds! the girl's mad!—her brain's turned by reading.

MRS. MALAPROP

O' my conscience, I believe so!—What do you mean by Beverley, hussy?—You saw Captain Absolute before today; there he is—your husband that shall be.

LYDIA

With all my soul, ma'am—when I refuse my Beverley——

SIR ANTHONY

Oh! she's as mad as Bedlam!—or has this fellow been playing us a rogue's trick!—Come here, sirrah, who the devil are you?

CAPTAIN ABSOLUTE

Faith, sir, I am not quite clear myself; but I'll endeavour to recollect.

SIR ANTHONY

Are you my son or not?—answer for your mother, you dog, if you won't for me.

MRS. MALAPROP

Ay, sir, who are you? O mercy! I begin to suspect!——

CAPTAIN ABSOLUTE

[*Aside.*] Ye powers of impudence, befriend me!— [*Aloud.*] Sir Anthony, most assuredly I am your wife's son; and that I sincerely believe myself to be yours also, I hope my duty has always shown.—Mrs. Malaprop, I am your most respectful admirer, and shall be proud to add affectionate nephew.—I need not tell my Lydia, that she sees her faithful Beverley, who, knowing the singular generosity of her temper, assumed that name and station, which has proved a test of the most disinterested love, which he now hopes to enjoy in a more elevated character.

LYDIA

So!—there will be no elopement after all!   [*Sullenly.*

SIR ANTHONY

Upon my soul, Jack, thou art a very impudent fellow! to do you justice, I think I never saw a piece of more consummate assurance!

CAPTAIN ABSOLUTE

Oh, you flatter me, sir—you compliment—'tis my modesty, you know, sir—my modesty that has stood in my way.

SIR ANTHONY

Well, I am glad you are not the dull, insensible varlet you pretended to be, however!—I'm glad you have made a fool of your father, you dog—I am. So this was your *penitence*, your *duty* and *obedience*!—I thought it was damned sudden!—*You never heard their names before*, not you!—*what, the Languishes of Worcestershire*, hey?—*if you could please me in the affair it was all you desired!*—Ah! you dissembling villain!—What!—[*Pointing to* LYDIA] *she squints don't she?—a little red-haired girl!*—hey?—Why, you hypo-critical young rascal!—I wonder you a'n't ashamed to hold up your head!

CAPTAIN ABSOLUTE

'Tis with difficulty, sir.—I am confused—very much confused, as you must perceive.

MRS. MALAPROP

O Lud! Sir Anthony!—a new light breaks in upon me!—hey!—how! what! captain, did you write the letters then?—What—am I to thank you for the elegant compilation of *an old weather-beaten she-dragon*—hey?—O mercy!—was it you that reflected on my parts of speech?

CAPTAIN ABSOLUTE

Dear sir! my modesty will be overpowered at last, if you don't assist me.—I shall certainly not be able to stand it!

SIR ANTHONY

Come, come, Mrs. Malaprop, we must forget and forgive;—odds life! matters have taken so clever a turn all of a sudden, that I could find in my heart to be so good-humoured! and so gallant! hey! Mrs. Malaprop!

MRS. MALAPROP

Well, Sir Anthony, since you desire it, we will not anticipate the past!—so mind, young people—our retrospection will be all to the future.

SIR ANTHONY

Come, we must leave them together; Mrs. Malaprop, they long to fly into each other's arms, I warrant!—Jack, isn't the cheek as I said, hey?—and the eye, you rogue?—and the lip—hey? Come, Mrs. Malaprop, we'll not disturb their tenderness—theirs is the time of life for happiness!—*Youth's the season made for joy*—[*Sings*]—hey!—Odds life! I'm in such spirits—I don't know what I could not do!—Permit me, ma'am—[*Gives his hand to* MRS. MALAPROP.]

Tol-de-rol—'gad, I should like to have a little fooling myself—Tol-de-rol! de-rol.

> [*Exit, singing and handing* MRS. MALAPROP. —LYDIA *sits sullenly in her chair.*

CAPTAIN ABSOLUTE

[*Aside.*] So much thought bodes me no good.— [*Aloud.*] So grave, Lydia!

LYDIA

Sir!

CAPTAIN ABSOLUTE

[*Aside.*] So!—egad! I thought as much!—that damned monosyllable has froze me!—[*Aloud.*] What, Lydia, now that we are as happy in our friends' consent, as in our mutual vows——

LYDIA

Friends' consent indeed!   [*Peevishly.*

CAPTAIN ABSOLUTE

Come, come, we must lay aside some of our romance —a little and comfort may be endured after all. And for your fortune, the lawyers shall make such settlements as——

LYDIA

Lawyers! I hate lawyers!

CAPTAIN ABSOLUTE

Nay, then, we will not wait for their lingering forms, but instantly procure the license, and——

LYDIA

The license!—I hate license!

CAPTAIN ABSOLUTE

Oh, my love! be not so unkind!—thus let me entreat——   [*Kneeling.*

LYDIA

Psha!—what signifies kneeling, when you know I must have you?

CAPTAIN ABSOLUTE

[*Rising.*] Nay, madam, there shall be no constraint upon your inclinations, I promise you.—If I have lost your heart—I resign the rest—[*Aside.*] 'Gad, I must try what a little spirit will do.

LYDIA

[*Rising.*] Then, sir, let me tell you, the interest you had there was acquired by a mean, unmanly imposition, and deserves the punishment of fraud.—What, you have been treating me like a child!—humouring my romance! and laughing, I suppose, at your success!

CAPTAIN ABSOLUTE

You wrong me, Lydia, you wrong me—only hear——

LYDIA

So, while I fondly imagined we were deceiving my relations, and flattered myself that I should outwit and incense them all—behold my hopes are to be crushed at once, by my aunt's consent and approbation—and I am myself the only dupe at last!—[*Walking about in a heat.*] But here, sir, here is the picture—Beverley's picture! [*taking a miniature from her bosom*] which I have worn, night and day, in spite of threats and entreaties!— There, sir; [*flings it to him*] and be assured I throw the original from my heart as easily.

CAPTAIN ABSOLUTE

Nay, nay, ma'am, we will not differ as to that.— Here, [*taking out a picture*] here is Miss Lydia

Languish.—What a difference!—ay, there is the
heavenly assenting smile that first gave soul and spirit
to my hopes!—those are the lips which sealed a vow,
as yet scarce dry in Cupid's calendar! and there the
half-resentful blush, that would have checked the
ardour of my thanks!—Well, all that's past?—all over
indeed!—There, madam—in beauty, that copy is not
equal to you, but in my mind its merit over the
original, in being still the same, is such—that—I cannot find in my heart to part with it. [*Puts it up again.*

LYDIA

[*Softening.*] 'Tis your own doing, sir—I, I, I suppose
you are perfectly satisfied.

CAPTAIN ABSOLUTE

O, most certainly—sure, now, this is much better
than being in love!—ha! ha! ha!—there's some spirit
in this!—What signifies breaking some scores of
solemn promises:—all that's of no consequence, you
know. To be sure people will say, that miss don't
know her own mind but never mind that! Or, perhaps, they may be ill-natured enough to hint, that the
gentleman grew tired of the lady and forsook her—
but don't let that fret you.

LYDIA

There is no bearing his insolence. [*Bursts into tears.*

Re-enter MRS. MALAPROP *and*
SIR ANTHONY ABSOLUTE

MRS. MALAPROP

Come, we must interrupt your billing and cooing
awhile.

LYDIA

This is worse than your treachery and deceit, you base ingrate!   [*Sobbing.*

SIR ANTHONY

What the devil's the matter now?—Zounds! Mrs. Malaprop, this is the oddest billing and cooing I ever heard!—but what the deuce is the meaning of it?—I am quite astonished!

CAPTAIN ABSOLUTE

Ask the lady, sir.

MRS. MALAPROP

O mercy!—I'm quite analyzed, for my part!—Why, Lydia, what is the reason of this?

LYDIA

Ask the gentleman, ma'am.

SIR ANTHONY

Zounds! I shall be in a frenzy!—Why, Jack, you are not come out to be any one else, are you?

MRS. MALAPROP

Ay, sir, there's no more trick, is there?—you are not like Cerberus, three gentlemen at once, are you?

CAPTAIN ABSOLUTE

You'll not let me speak—I say the lady can account for this much better than I can.

LYDIA

Ma'am, you once commanded me never to think of Beverley again—there is the man—I now obey you: for, from this moment, I renounce him for ever.

[*Exit.*

MRS. MALAPROP

O mercy! and miracles! what a turn here is—why,

CAPTAIN ABSOLUTE

sure, captain, you haven't behaved disrespectfully to my niece?

SIR ANTHONY

Ha! ha! ha!—ha! ha! ha!—now I see it. Ha! ha! ha! —now I see it—you have been too lively, Jack.

CAPTAIN ABSOLUTE

Nay, sir, upon my word——

SIR ANTHONY

Come, no lying, Jack—I'm sure 'twas so.

MRS. MALAPROP

O Lud! Sir Anthony!—O fy, captain!

CAPTAIN ABSOLUTE

Upon my soul, ma'am——

SIR ANTHONY

Come, no excuse, Jack; why, your father, you rogue, was so before you!—the blood of the Absolutes was always impatient.—Ha! ha! ha! poor little Lydia! why, you've frightened her, you dog, you have.

CAPTAIN ABSOLUTE

By all that's good, sir——

SIR ANTHONY

Zounds! say no more, I tell you, Mrs. Malaprop shall make your peace. You must make his peace, Mrs. Malaprop:—you must tell her 'tis Jack's way—tell her 'tis all our ways—it runs in the blood of our family! Come away, Jack. Ha! ha! ha!—Mrs. Malaprop—a young villain! [*Pushing him out.*

MRS. MALAPROP

O! Sir Anthony!—O fy, captain! [*Exeunt severally.*

SCENE THREE

The North Parade

Enter SIR LUCIUS O'TRIGGER

SIR LUCIUS

I wonder where this Captain Absolute hides himself!
Upon my conscience! these officers are always in one's
way in love affairs:—I remember I might have
married Lady Dorothy Carmine, if it had not been
for a little rogue of a major, who ran away with her
before she could get a sight of me! And I wonder too
what it is the ladies can see in them to be so fond of
them—unless it be a touch of the old serpent in 'em,
that makes the little creatures be caught, like vipers,
with a bit of red cloth. Ha! isn't this the captain
coming?—faith it is!—There is a probability of suc-
ceeding about that fellow, that is mighty provoking!
Who the devil is he talking to?   [*Steps aside.*

Enter CAPTAIN ABSOLUTE

CAPTAIN ABSOLUTE

[*Aside.*] To what fine purpose I have been plotting!
a noble reward for all my schemes, upon my soul!—
a little gipsy!—I did not think her romance could
have made her so damned absurd either. 'Sdeath, I
never was in a worse humour in my life!—I could cut
my own throat, or any other person's with the greatest
pleasure in the world!

SIR LUCIUS

Oh, faith! I'm in the luck of it. I never could have
found him in a sweeter temper for my purpose—to be

sure I'm just come in the nick! Now to enter into conversation with him, and so quarrel genteelly.— [*Goes up to* CAPTAIN ABSOLUTE.] With regard to that matter, captain, I must beg leave to differ in opinion with you.

CAPTAIN ABSOLUTE

Upon my word, then, you must be a very subtle disputant:—because, sir, I happened just then to be giving no opinion at all.

SIR LUCIUS

That's no reason. For give me leave to tell you, a man may think an untruth as well as speak one.

CAPTAIN ABSOLUTE

Very true, sir; but if a man never utters his thoughts, I should think they might stand a chance of escaping controversy.

SIR LUCIUS

Then, sir, you differ in opinion with me, which amounts to the same thing.

CAPTAIN ABSOLUTE

Hark'ee, Sir Lucius; if I had not before known you to be a gentleman, upon my soul, I should not have discovered it at this interview: for what you can drive at, unless you mean to quarrel with me, I cannot conceive!

SIR LUCIUS

I humbly thank you, sir, for the quickness of your apprehension.—[*Bowing*.] You have named the very thing I would be at.

CAPTAIN ABSOLUTE

Very well, sir; I shall certainly not balk your

inclinations.—But I should be glad you would be pleased to explain your motives.

SIR LUCIUS

Pray, sir, be easy; the quarrel is a very pretty quarrel as it stands; we should only spoil it by trying to explain it. However, your memory is very short, or you could not have forgot an affront you passed on me within this week. So, no more, but name your time and place.

CAPTAIN ABSOLUTE

Well, sir, since you are so bent on it, the sooner the better; let it be this evening—here, by the Spring Gardens. We shall scarcely be interrupted.

SIR LUCIUS

Faith! that same interruption in affairs of this nature shows very great ill-breeding. I don't know what's the reason, but in England if a thing of this kind gets wind, people make such a pother, that a gentleman can never fight in peace and quietness. However, if it's the same to you, I should take it as a particular kindness if you'd let us meet in King's-Mead-Fields, as a little business will call me there about six o'clock, and I may despatch both matters at once.

CAPTAIN ABSOLUTE

'Tis the same to me exactly. A little after six, then, we will discuss this matter more seriously.

SIR LUCIUS

If you please, sir; there will be very pretty small-sword light, though it won't do for a long shot. So that matter's settled, and my mind's at ease! [*Exit.*

Enter FAULKLAND

CAPTAIN ABSOLUTE

Well met! I was going to look for you. O Faulkland! all the demons of spite and disappointment have conspired against me! I'm so vex'd, that if I had not the prospect of a resource in being knocked o' the head by-and-by, I should scarce have spirits to tell you the cause.

FAULKLAND

What can you mean?—Has Lydia changed her mind? —I should have thought her duty and inclination would now have pointed to the same object.

CAPTAIN ABSOLUTE

Ay, just as the eyes do of a person who squints: when her love-eye was fixed on me, t'other, her eye of duty, was finely obliqued: but when duty bid her point that the same way, off t'other turned on a swivel, and secured its retreat with a frown!

FAULKLAND

But what's the resource you——

CAPTAIN ABSOLUTE

Oh, to wind up the whole, a good-natured Irishman here has—[*Mimicking* SIR LUCIUS] begged leave to have the pleasure of cutting my throat; and I mean to indulge him—that's all.

FAULKLAND

Prithee, be serious!

CAPTAIN ABSOLUTE

'Tis fact, upon my soul! Sir Lucius O'Trigger—you know him by sight—for some affront, which I am sure I never intended, has obliged me to meet him this evening at six o'clock: 'tis on that account I wished to see you; you must go with me.

FAULKLAND

Nay, there must be some mistake, sure. Sir Lucius shall explain himself, and I dare say matters may be accommodated. But this evening did you say? I wish it had been any other time.

CAPTAIN ABSOLUTE

Why? there will be light enough: there will (as Sir Lucius says) be very pretty small-sword light, though it will not do for a long shot. Confound his long shots.

FAULKLAND

But I am myself a good deal ruffled by a difference I have had with Julia. My vile tormenting temper has made me treat her so cruelly, that I shall not be myself till we are reconciled.

CAPTAIN ABSOLUTE

By heavens! Faulkland, you don't deserve her!

Enter SERVANT, *gives* FAULKLAND *a letter, and exit*

FAULKLAND

Oh, Jack! this is from Julia. I dread to open it! I fear it may be to take a last leave!—perhaps to bid me return her letters, and restore——Oh, how I suffer for my folly!

CAPTAIN ABSOLUTE

Here, let me see.—[*Takes the letter and opens it.*] Ay, a final sentence, indeed!—'tis all over with you, faith!

FAULKLAND

Nay, Jack, don't keep me in suspense!

CAPTAIN ABSOLUTE

Hear then—[*Reads.*] *As I am convinced that my dear Faulkland's own reflections have already upbraided him*

126

for his last unkindness to me, I will not add a word on *the subject. I wish to speak with you as soon as possible.* *Yours ever and truly,* JULIA. There's stubbornness and resentment for you!—[*Gives him the letter.*] Why, man, you don't seem one whit happier at this!

FAULKLAND

O yes, I am; but—but—

CAPTAIN ABSOLUTE

Confound your buts! you never hear anything that would make another man bless himself, but you immediately damn it with a but!

FAULKLAND

Now, Jack, as you are my friend, own honestly— don't you think there is something forward, something indelicate, in this haste to forgive? Women should never sue for reconciliation: that should always come from us. They should retain their coldness till wooed to kindness; and their pardon, like their love, should 'not unsought be won.'

CAPTAIN ABSOLUTE

I have not patience to listen to you! thou'rt incorrigible! so say no more on the subject. I must go to settle a few matters. Let me see you before six, remember, at my lodgings. A poor industrious devil like me, who have toiled, and drudged, and plotted to gain my ends, and am at last disappointed by other people's folly, may in pity be allowed to swear and grumble a little; but a captious sceptic in love, a slave to fretfulness and whim, who has no difficulties but of his own creating, is a subject more fit for ridicule than compassion! [*Exit.*

FAULKLAND

I feel his reproaches; yet I would not change this too exquisite nicety for the gross content with which he tramples on the thorns of love! His engaging me in this duel has started an idea in my head, which I will instantly pursue. I'll use it as the touch-stone of Julia's sincerity and disinterestedness. If her love proves pure and sterling ore, my name will rest on it with honour; and once I've stamped it there, I lay aside my doubts for ever! But if the dross of selfishness, the alloy of pride, predominate, 'twill be best to leave her as a toy for some less cautious fool to sigh for! [*Exit.*

FAULKLAND

ACT FIVE

SCENE ONE

JULIA's *Dressing-Room*

JULIA *discovered alone*

JULIA

How this message has alarmed me! what dreadful accident can he mean? why such charge to be alone? —O Faulkland!—how many unhappy moments— how many tears have you cost me.

Enter FAULKLAND

JULIA

What means this?—why this caution, Faulkland?

FAULKLAND

Alas! Julia, I am come to take a long farewell.

JULIA

Heavens! what do you mean?

FAULKLAND

You see before you a wretch, whose life is forfeited. Nay, start not!—the infirmity of my temper has drawn all this misery on me. I left you fretful and passionate—an untoward accident drew me into a quarrel—the event is, that I must fly this kingdom instantly. O Julia, had I been so fortunate as to have called you mine entirely, before this mischance had fallen on me, I should not so deeply dread my banishment!

JULIA

My soul is opprest with sorrow at the nature of your
misfortune: had these adverse circumstances arisen
from a less fatal cause I should have felt strong comfort in the thought that I could now chase from your
bosom every doubt of the warm sincerity of my love.
My heart has long known no other guardian—I now
entrust my person to your honour—we will fly together. When safe from pursuit, my father's will may
be fulfilled—and I receive a legal claim to be the partner of your sorrows, and tenderest comforter. Then on
the bosom of your wedded Julia, you may lull your
keen regret to slumbering, while virtuous love, with a
cherub's hand, shall smoothe the brow of upbraiding
thought, and pluck the thorn from compunction.

FAULKLAND

O Julia! I am bankrupt in gratitude! but the time is
so pressing, it calls on you for so hasty a resolution.—
Would you not wish some hours to weigh the advan-
tages you forego, and what little compensation poor
Faulkland can make you beside his solitary love?

JULIA

I ask not a moment. No, Faulkland, I have loved you
for yourself: and if I now, more than ever, prize the
solemn engagement which so long has pledged us to
each other, it is because it leaves no room for hard
aspersions on my fame, and puts the seal of duty to
an act of love. But let us not linger. Perhaps this
delay——

FAULKLAND

'Twill be better I should not venture out again till

dark. Yet am I grieved to think what numberless distresses will press heavy on your gentle disposition!

JULIA

Perhaps your fortune may be forfeited by this unhappy act.—I know not whether 'tis so; but sure that alone can never make us unhappy. The little I have will be sufficient to support us; and exile never should be splendid.

FAULKLAND

Ay, but in such an abject state of life, my wounded pride perhaps may increase the natural fretfulness of my temper, till I become a rude, morose companion, beyond your patience to endure. Perhaps the recollection of a deed my conscience cannot justify may haunt me in such gloomy and unsocial fits, that I shall hate the tenderness that would relieve me, break from your arms, and quarrel with your fondness!

JULIA

If your thoughts should assume so unhappy a bent, you will the more want some mild and affectionate spirit to watch over and console you! one who, by bearing your infirmities with gentleness and resignation, may teach you so to bear the evils of your fortune.

FAULKLAND

Julia, I have proved you to the quick! and with this useless device I throw away all my doubts. How shall I plead to be forgiven this last unworthy effect of my restless, unsatisfied disposition?

JULIA

Has no such disaster happened as you related?

FAULKLAND

I am ashamed to own that it was pretended; yet in pity, Julia, do not kill me with resenting a fault which never can be repeated: but sealing, this once, my pardon, let me tomorrow, in the face of Heaven, receive my future guide and monitress, and expiate my past folly by years of tender adoration.

JULIA

Hold, Faulkland!—that you are free from a crime, which I before feared to name, Heaven knows how sincerely I rejoice! These are tears of thankfulness for that! But that your cruel doubts should have urged you to an imposition that has wrung my heart, gives me now a pang more keen than I can express.

FAULKLAND

By Heavens! Julia——

JULIA

Yet hear me,—My father loved you, Faulkland! and you preserved the life that tender parent gave me; in his presence I pledged my hand—joyfully pledged it —where before I had given my heart. When, soon after, I lost that parent, it seemed to me that Providence had, in Faulkland, shown me whither to transfer without a pause, my grateful duty, as well as my affection; hence I have been content to bear from you what pride and delicacy would have forbid me from another. I will not upbraid you, by repeating how you have trifled with my sincerity——

FAULKLAND

I confess it all! yet hear——

JULIA

After such a year of trial, I might have flattered

myself that I should not have been insulted with a new probation of my sincerity, as cruel as unnecessary! I now see it is not in your nature to be content or confident in love. With this conviction—I never will be yours. While I had hopes that my persevering attention, and unreproaching kindness, might in time reform your temper, I should have been happy to have gained a dearer influence over you; but I will not furnish you with a licensed power to keep alive an incorrigible fault, at the expense of one who never would contend with you.

FAULKLAND

Nay, but, Julia, by my soul and honour, if after this——

JULIA

But one word more.—As my faith has once been given to you, I never will barter it with another.—I shall pray for your happiness with the truest sincerity; and the dearest blessing I can ask of Heaven to send you will be to charm you from that unhappy temper, which alone has prevented the performance of our solemn engagement. All I request of you is, that you will yourself reflect upon this infirmity, and when you number up the many true delights it has deprived you of, let it not be your least regret, that it lost you the love of one who would have followed you in beggary through the world! 					[*Exit.*

FAULKLAND

She's gone—for ever!—There was an awful resolution in her manner, that riveted me to my place.—O fool!—dolt!—barbarian! Cursed as I am, with more imperfections than my fellow-wretches, kind Fortune

133

sent a heaven-gifted cherub to my aid, and, like a ruffian, I have driven her from my side!—I must now haste to my appointment. Well, my mind is tuned for such a scene. I shall wish only to become a principal in it, and reverse the tale my cursed folly put me upon forging here.—O Love!—tormentor!—fiend!—whose influence, like the moon's, acting on men of dull souls, makes idiots of them, but meeting subtler spirits, betrays their course, and urges sensibility to madness!

[*Exit.*

Enter LYDIA *and* MAID

MAID

My mistress, ma'am, I know, was here just now— perhaps she is only in the next room.   [*Exit.*

LYDIA

Heigh-ho! Though he has used me so, this fellow runs strangely in my head. I believe one lecture from my grave cousin will make me recall him. [*Re-enter* JULIA.] O Julia, I have come to you with such an appetite for consolation.—Lud! child, what's the matter with you? You have been crying!—I'll be hanged if that Faulkland has not been tormenting you.

JULIA

You mistake the cause of my uneasiness!—Something has flurried me a little. Nothing that you can guess at.—[*Aside.*] I would not accuse Faulkland to a sister!

LYDIA

Ah! whatever vexations you may have, I can assure you mine surpass them. You know who Beverley proves to be?

134

JULIA

I will now own to you, Lydia, that Mr. Faulkland had before informed me of the whole affair. Had young Absolute been the person you took him for, I should not have accepted your confidence on the subject, without a serious endeavour to counteract your caprice.

LYDIA

So, then, I see I have been deceived by every one! But I don't care—I'll never have him.

JULIA

Nay, Lydia——

LYDIA

Why, is it not provoking? when I thought we were coming to the prettiest distress imaginable, to find myself made a mere Smithfield bargain of at last! There, had I projected one of the most sentimental elopements!—so becoming a disguise!—so amiable a ladder of ropes!—Conscious moon—four horses—Scotch parson—with such surprise to Mrs. Malaprop —and such paragraphs in the newspapers!—Oh, I shall die with disappointment!

JULIA

I don't wonder at it!

LYDIA

Now—sad reverse!—what have I to expect, but, after a deal of flimsy preparation, with a bishop's license, and my aunt's blessing, to go simpering up to the altar; or perhaps be cried three times in a country church, and have an unmannerly fat clerk ask the consent of every butcher in the parish to join John

Absolute and Lydia Languish, spinster! Oh that I should live to hear myself called spinster!

JULIA

Melancholy, indeed!

LYDIA

How mortifying, to remember the dear delicious shifts I used to be put to, to gain half a minute's conversation with this fellow! How often have I stole forth, in the coldest night in January, and found him in the garden, stuck like a dripping statue! There would he kneel to me in the snow, and sneeze and cough so pathetically! he shivering with cold and I with apprehension! and while the freezing blast numbed our joints, how warmly would he press me to pity his flame, and glow with mutual ardour!—Ah, Julia, that was something like being in love.

JULIA

If I were in spirits, Lydia, I should chide you only by laughing heartily at you; but it suits more the situation of my mind, at present, earnestly to entreat you not to let a man, who loves you with sincerity, suffer that unhappiness from your caprice, which I know too well caprice can inflict.

LYDIA

O Lud! what has brought my aunt here?

Enter MRS. MALAPROP, FAG, *and* DAVID

MRS. MALAPROP

So! so! here's fine work!—here's fine suicide, parricide, and simulation, going on in the fields! and Sir Anthony not to be found to prevent the antistrophe!

136

JULIA

For Heaven's sake, madam, what's the meaning of this?

MRS. MALAPROP

That gentleman can tell you—'twas he enveloped the affair to me.

LYDIA

Do, sir, will you, inform us?   [*To* FAG.

FAG

Ma'am, I should hold myself very deficient in every requisite that forms the man of breeding, if I delayed a moment to give all the information in my power to a lady so deeply interested in the affair as you are.

LYDIA

But quick! quick, sir!

FAG

True, ma'am, as you say, one should be quick in divulging matters of this nature; for should we be tedious, perhaps while we are flourishing on the subject, two or three lives may be lost!

LYDIA

O patience!—do, ma'am, for Heaven's sake! tell us what is the matter?

MRS. MALAPROP

Why, murder's the matter! slaughter's the matter! killing's the matter!—but he can tell you the perpendiculars.

LYDIA

Then, prithee, sir, be brief.

FAG

Why, then, ma'am, as to murder—I cannot take upon

137

me to say—and as to slaughter, or manslaughter, that will be as the jury finds it.

LYDIA
But who, sir—who are engaged in this?

FAG
Faith, ma'am, one is a young gentleman whom I should be very sorry anything was to happen to—a very pretty behaved gentleman! We have lived much together, and always on terms.

LYDIA
But who is this? who? who? who?

FAG
My master, ma'am—my master—I speak of my master.

LYDIA
Heavens! What, Captain Absolute!

MRS. MALAPROP
Oh, to be sure, you are frightened now!

JULIA
But who are with him, sir?

FAG
As to the rest, ma'am, this gentleman can inform you better than I.

JULIA
Do speak, friend. [*To* DAVID.

DAVID
Look'ee, my lady—by the mass! there's mischief going on. Folks don't use to meet for amusement with fire-arms, firelocks, fire-engines, fire-screens, fire-office, and the devil knows what other crackers beside!—This, my lady, I say, has an angry savour.

JULIA

But who is there beside Captain Absolute, friend?

DAVID

My poor master—under favour for mentioning him first. You know me, my lady—I am David—and my master of course is, or was, Squire Acres. Then comes Squire Faulkland.

JULIA

Do, ma'am, let us instantly endeavour to prevent mischief.

MRS. MALAPROP

O fy! it would be very inelegant in us:—we should only participate things.

DAVID

Ah! do, Mrs. Aunt, save a few lives—they are desperately given, believe me.—Above all, there is that bloodthirsty Philistine, Sir Lucius O'Trigger.

MRS. MALAPROP

Sir Lucius O'Trigger? O mercy! have they drawn poor little dear Sir Lucius into the scrape? Why how you stand, girl! you have no more feeling than one of the Derbyshire petrifactions!

LYDIA

What are we to do, madam?

MRS. MALAPROP

Why, fly with the utmost felicity, to be sure, to prevent mischief!—Here, friend, you can show us the place?

FAG

If you please, ma'am, I will conduct you.—David, do you look for Sir Anthony.   [*Exit* DAVID.

MRS. MALAPROP

Come, girls! this gentleman will exhort us.—Come,
sir, you're our envoy—lead the way, and we'll precede.

FAG

Not a step before the ladies for the world!

MRS. MALAPROP

You're sure you know the spot?

FAG

I think I can find it, ma'am; and one good thing is,
we shall hear the report of the pistols as we draw near,
so we can't well miss them;—never fear, ma'am,
never fear.   [*Exeunt, he talking.*

SCENE TWO

The South Parade

Enter CAPTAIN ABSOLUTE, *putting his sword
under his great-coat.*

CAPTAIN ABSOLUTE

A sword seen in the streets of Bath would raise as
great an alarm as a mad dog.—How provoking this is
in Faulkland!—never punctual! I shall be obliged to
go without him at last.—Oh, the devil! here's Sir
Anthony! how shall I escape him?
        [*Muffles up his face, and takes a circle to go off.*

Enter SIR ANTHONY ABSOLUTE

SIR ANTHONY

How one may be deceived at a little distance! Only

that I see he don't know me, I could have sworn that was Jack!—Hey! Gad's life! it is.—Why, Jack, what are you afraid of? hey—sure I'm right. Why, Jack, Jack Absolute!   [*Goes up to him.*

CAPTAIN ABSOLUTE

Really, sir, you have the advantage of me:—I don't remember ever to have had the honour—my name is Saunderson, at your service.

SIR ANTHONY

Sir, I beg your pardon—I took you—hey?—why, zounds! it is—Stay—[*Looks up to his face.*] So, so—your humble servant, Mr. Saunderson! Why, you scoundrel, what tricks are you after now?

CAPTAIN ABSOLUTE

Oh, a joke, sir, a joke! I came here on purpose to look for you, sir.

SIR ANTHONY

You did! well, I am glad you were so lucky:—but what are you muffled up so for?—what's this for?—hey?

CAPTAIN ABSOLUTE

'Tis cool, sir, isn't it?—rather chilly somehow:—but I shall be late—I have a particular engagement.

SIR ANTHONY

Stay!—Why, I thought you were looking for me?—Pray, Jack, where is't you are going?

CAPTAIN ABSOLUTE

Going, sir?

SIR ANTHONY

Ay, where are you going?

CAPTAIN ABSOLUTE

Where am I going?

SIR ANTHONY

You unmannerly puppy!

CAPTAIN ABSOLUTE

I was going, sir, to—to—to—to Lydia—sir, to Lydia
—to make matters up if I could; and I was looking
for you, sir, to—to—

SIR ANTHONY

To go with you, I suppose.—Well, come along.

CAPTAIN ABSOLUTE

Oh! zounds! no, sir, not for the world!—I wished to
meet with you, sir,—to—to—to—You find it cool,
I'm sure, sir—you'd better not stay out.

SIR ANTHONY

Cool!—not at all.—Well, Jack—and what will you
say to Lydia?

CAPTAIN ABSOLUTE

Oh, sir, beg her pardon, humour her—promise and
vow: but I detain you, sir—consider the cold air on
your gout.

SIR ANTHONY

Oh, not at all!—not at all! I'm in no hurry.—Ah!
Jack, you youngsters, when once you are wounded
here [*Putting his hand to* CAPTAIN ABSOLUTE'S
breast.] Hey! what the deuce have you got here?

CAPTAIN ABSOLUTE

Nothing, sir—nothing.

SIR ANTHONY

What's this?—here's something damned hard.

CAPTAIN ABSOLUTE

Oh, trinkets, sir! trinkets!—a bauble for Lydia.

SIR ANTHONY

Nay, let me see your taste.—[*Pulls his coat open, the sword falls.*] Trinkets! a bauble for Lydia!—Zounds! sirrah, you are not going to cut her throat, are you?

CAPTAIN ABSOLUTE

Ha! ha! ha!—I thought it would divert you, sir, though I didn't mean to tell you till afterwards.

SIR ANTHONY

You didn't?—Yes, this is a very diverting trinket, truly!

CAPTAIN ABSOLUTE

Sir, I'll explain to you.—You know, sir, Lydia is romantic, devilish romantic, and very absurd of course: now, sir, I intend, if she refuses to forgive me, to unsheath this sword, and swear—I'll fall upon its point, and expire at her feet!

SIR ANTHONY

Fall upon a fiddlestick's end!—why, I suppose it is the very thing that would please her.—Get along, you fool!

CAPTAIN ABSOLUTE

Well, sir, you shall hear of my success—you shall hear.—*O Lydia!—forgive me, or this pointed steel*—says I.

SIR ANTHONY

O, booby! stay away and welcome—says she.—Get along! and damn your trinkets!

[*Exit* CAPTAIN ABSOLUTE.

Enter DAVID, *running*

143

DAVID

Stop him! stop him! Murder! Thief! Fire!—Stop fire! Stop fire!—O Sir Anthony—call! call! bid'm stop! Murder! Fire!

SIR ANTHONY

Fire! Murder!—Where?

DAVID

Oons! he's out of sight! and I'm out of breath for my part! O Sir Anthony, why didn't you stop him? why didn't you stop him?

SIR ANTHONY

Zounds! the fellow's mad!—Stop whom? stop Jack?

DAVID

Ay, the captain, sir!—there's murder and slaughter——

SIR ANTHONY

Murder!

DAVID

Ay, please you, Sir Anthony, there's all kinds of murder, all sorts of slaughter to be seen in the fields: there's fighting going on, sir—bloody sword-and-gun fighting!

SIR ANTHONY

Who are going to fight, dunce?

DAVID

Everybody that I know of, Sir Anthony:—everybody is going to fight, my poor master, Sir Lucius O'Trigger, your son, the captain——

SIR ANTHONY

Oh, the dog! I see his tricks.—Do you know the place?

DAVID

King's-Mead-Fields.

SIR ANTHONY

You know the way?

DAVID

Not an inch; but I'll call the mayor—aldermen—constables—churchwardens—and beadles—we can't be too many to part them.

SIR ANTHONY

Come along—give me your shoulder! we'll get assistance as we go—the lying villain!—Well, I shall be in such a frenzy!—So—this was the history of his trinkets! I'll bauble him!   [*Exeunt.*

SCENE THREE

King's-Mead-Fields

Enter SIR LUCIUS O'TRIGGER *and* ACRES, *with pistols*

ACRES

By my valour! then, Sir Lucius, forty yards is a good distance. Odds levels and aims!—I say it is a good distance.

SIR LUCIUS

Is it for muskets or small field-pieces? Upon my conscience, Mr. Acres, you must leave those things to me.—Stay now—I'll show you.—[*Measures paces along the stage.*] There now, that is a very pretty distance—a pretty gentleman's distance.

ACRES

Zounds! we might as well fight in a sentry-box! I tell you, Sir Lucius, the farther he is off, the cooler I shall take my aim.

SIR LUCIUS

Faith! then I suppose you would aim at him best of all if he was out of sight!

ACRES

No, Sir Lucius; but I should think forty or eight and thirty yards——

SIR LUCIUS

Pho! pho! nonsense! three or four feet between the mouths of your pistols is as good as a mile.

ACRES

Odds bullets, no!—by my valour! there is no merit in killing him so near; do, my dear Sir Lucius, let me bring him down at a long shot—a long shot, Sir Lucius, if you love me.

SIR LUCIUS

Well, the gentleman's friend and I must settle that.— But tell me now, Mr. Acres, in case of an accident, is there any little will or commission I could execute for you?

ACRES

I am much obliged to you, Sir Lucius, but I don't understand——

SIR LUCIUS

Why, you may think there's no being shot at without a little risk—and if an unlucky bullet should carry a quietus with it—I say it will be no time then to be bothering you about family matters.

ACRES

A quietus!

SIR LUCIUS

For instance, now—if that should be the case—would you choose to be pickled and sent home?—or would it be the same to you to lie here in the Abbey? I'm told there is very snug lying in the Abbey.

ACRES

Pickled!—Snug lying in the Abbey!—Odds tremors! Sir Lucius, don't talk so!

SIR LUCIUS

I suppose, Mr. Acres, you never were engaged in an affair of this kind before?

ACRES

No, Sir Lucius, never before.

SIR LUCIUS

Ah! that's a pity!—there's nothing like being used to a thing. Pray now, how would you receive the gentleman's shot?

ACRES

Odds files!—I've practised that—there, Sir Lucius— there. [*Puts himself in an attitude.*] A side-front, hey? Odd! I'll make myself small enough? I'll stand edgeways.

SIR LUCIUS

Now—you're quite out—for if you stand so when I take my aim——   [*Levelling at him.*

ACRES

Zounds! Sir Lucius—are you sure it is not cocked?

SIR LUCIUS

Never fear.

147

ACRES

But—but—you don't know—it may go off of its own head!

SIR LUCIUS

Pho! be easy.—Well, now if I hit you in the body, my bullet has a double chance—for if it misses a vital part of your right side, 'twill be very hard if it don't succeed on the left!

ACRES

A vital part.

SIR LUCIUS

But, there—fix yourself so—[*Placing him*]—let him see the broad-side of your full front—there—now a ball or two may pass clean through your body, and never do any harm at all.

ACRES

Clean through me!—a ball or two clean through me!

SIR LUCIUS

Ay—may they—and it is much the genteelest attitude into the bargain.

ACRES

Look'ee! Sir Lucius—I'd just as lieve be shot in an awkward posture as a genteel one; so, by my valour! I will stand edgeways.

SIR LUCIUS

[*Looking at his watch.*] Sure they don't mean to disappoint us—Hah!—no, faith—I think I see them coming.

ACRES

Hey!—what!—coming!——

SIR LUCIUS

Ay.—Who are those yonder getting over the stile?

ACRES

There are two of them indeed!—well—let them come —hey, Sir Lucius!—we—we—we—we—won't run.

SIR LUCIUS

Run!

ACRES

No—I say—we won't run, by my valour!

SIR LUCIUS

What the devil's the matter with you?

ACRES

Nothing—nothing—my dear friend—my dear Sir Lucius—but I—I—I don't feel quite so bold, somehow, as I did.

SIR LUCIUS

O fy!—consider your honour.

ACRES

Ay—true—my honour. Do, Sir Lucius, edge in a word or two every now and then about my honour.

SIR LUCIUS

Well, here they're coming.   [*Looking.*

ACRES

Sir Lucius—if I wa'n't with you, I should almost think I was afraid.—If my valour should leave me! Valour will come and go.

SIR LUCIUS

Then pray keep it fast, while you have it.

ACRES

Sir Lucius—I doubt it is going—yes—my valour is

149

certainly going!—it is sneaking off!—I feel it oozing out as it were at the palms of my hands!

SIR LUCIUS

Your honour—your honour.—Here they are.

ACRES

O mercy!—now—that I was safe at Clod Hall! or could be shot before I was aware!

Enter FAULKLAND *and* CAPTAIN ABSOLUTE

SIR LUCIUS

Gentlemen, your most obedient.—Hah!—what, Captain Absolute!—So, I suppose, sir, you are come here, just like myself—to do a kind office, first for your friend—then to proceed to business on your own account.

ACRES

What, Jack!—my dear Jack!—my dear friend!

CAPTAIN ABSOLUTE

Hark'ee, Bob, Beverley's at hand.

SIR LUCIUS

Well, Mr. Acres—I don't blame your saluting the gentleman civilly.—[*To* FAULKLAND.] So, Mr. Beverley, if you'll choose your weapons, the captain and I will measure the ground.

FAULKLAND

My weapons, sir!

ACRES

Odds life! Sir Lucius, I'm not going to fight Mr. Faulkland; these are my particular friends.

SIR LUCIUS

What, sir, did you not come here to fight Mr. Acres?

FAULKLAND

Not I, upon my word, sir.

SIR LUCIUS

Well, now, that's mighty provoking! But I hope, Mr. Faulkland, as there are three of us come on purpose for the game, you won't be so cantankerous as to spoil the party by sitting out.

CAPTAIN ABSOLUTE

O pray, Faulkland, fight to oblige Sir Lucius.

FAULKLAND

Nay, if Mr. Acres is so bent on the matter——

ACRES

No, no, Mr. Faulkland;—I'll bear my disappointment like a Christian.—Look'ee, Sir Lucius, there's no occasion at all for me to fight; and if it is the same to you, I'd as lieve let it alone.

SIR LUCIUS

Observe me, Mr. Acres—I must not be trifled with. You have certainly challenged somebody—and you came here to fight him. Now, if that gentleman is willing to represent him—I can't see, for my soul, why it isn't just the same thing.

ACRES

Why no—Sir Lucius—I tell you, 'tis one Beverley I've challenged—a fellow, you see, that dare not show his face!—if he were here, I'd make him give up his pretensions directly!

CAPTAIN ABSOLUTE

Hold, Bob—let me set you right—there is no such man as Beverley in the case.—The person who

assumed that name is before you; and as his pretensions are the same in both characters, he is ready to
support them in whatever way you please.

SIR LUCIUS

Well, this is lucky.—Now you have an opportunity—

ACRES

What, quarrel with my dear friend, Jack Absolute?—
not if he were fifty Beverleys! Zounds! Sir Lucius,
you would not have me so unnatural.

SIR LUCIUS

Upon my conscience, Mr. Acres, your valour has
oozed away with a vengeance!

ACRES

Not in the least! Odds backs and abettors! I'll be your
second with all my heart—and if you should get a
quietus, you may command me entirely. I'll get you
snug lying in the Abbey here; or pickle you, and send
you over to Blunderbuss-hall, or anything of the kind,
with the greatest pleasure.

SIR LUCIUS

Pho! pho! you are little better than a coward.

ACRES

Mind, gentlemen, he calls me a coward; coward was
the word, by my valour!

SIR LUCIUS

Well, sir?

ACRES

Look'ee, Sir Lucius, 'tisn't that I mind the word
coward—coward may be said in joke.—But if you had
called me a poltroon, odds daggers and balls——

LYDIA LANGUISH

SIR LUCIUS
Well, sir?

ACRES
I should have thought you a very ill-bred man.

SIR LUCIUS
Pho! you are beneath my notice.

CAPTAIN ABSOLUTE
Nay, Sir Lucius, you can't have a better second than
my friend Acres.—He is a most determined dog—
called in the country, Fighting Bob.—He generally
kills a man a week—don't you, Bob?

ACRES
Ay—at home!

SIR LUCIUS
Well, then, captain, 'tis we must begin—so come out,
my little counsellor—[*Draws his sword*]—and ask the
gentleman, whether he will resign the lady, without
forcing you to proceed against him?

CAPTAIN ABSOLUTE
Come on then, sir—[*Draws*]; since you won't let it be
an amicable suit, here's my reply.

Enter SIR ANTHONY ABSOLUTE, DAVID,
MRS. MALAPROP, LYDIA, *and* JULIA

DAVID
Knock 'em all down, sweet Sir Anthony; knock down
my master in particular; and bind his hands over to
their good behaviour!

SIR ANTHONY
Put up, Jack, put up, or I shall be in a frenzy—how
came you in a duel, sir?

CAPTAIN ABSOLUTE

Faith, sir, that gentleman can tell you better than I; 'twas he called on me, and you know, sir, I serve his majesty.

SIR ANTHONY

Here's a pretty fellow; I catch him going to cut a man's throat, and he tells me he serves his majesty!— Zounds! sirrah, then how durst you draw the king's sword against one of his subjects?

CAPTAIN ABSOLUTE

Sir! I tell you, that gentleman called me out, without explaining his reasons.

SIR ANTHONY

Gad! sir, how came you to call my son out, without explaining your reasons?

SIR LUCIUS

Your son, sir, insulted me in a manner which my honour could not brook.

SIR ANTHONY

Zounds! Jack, how durst you insult the gentleman in a manner which his honour could not brook?

MRS. MALAPROP

Come, come, let's have no honour before ladies— Captain Absolute, come here—How could you intimidate us so?—Here's Lydia has been terrified to death for you.

CAPTAIN ABSOLUTE

For fear I should be killed, or escape, ma'am?

MRS. MALAPROP

Nay, no delusions to the past—Lydia is convinced; speak, child.

154

SIR LUCIUS

With your leave, ma'am, I must put in a word, here:
I believe I could interpret the young lady's silence.
Now mark——

LYDIA

What is it you mean, sir?

SIR LUCIUS

Come, come, Delia, we must be serious now—this is
no time for trifling.

LYDIA

'Tis true, sir; and your reproof bids me offer this
gentleman my hand, and solicit the return of his
affections.

CAPTAIN ABSOLUTE

O! my little angel, say you so?—Sir Lucius, I perceive
there must be some mistake here, with regard to the
affront which you affirm I have given you. I can only
say that it could not have been intentional. And as
you must be convinced, that I should not fear to support a real injury—you shall now see that I am not
ashamed to atone for an inadvertency—I ask your
pardon.—But for this lady, while honoured with her
approbation, I will support my claim against any man
whatever.

SIR ANTHONY

Well said, Jack, and I'll stand by you, my boy.

ACRES

Mind, I give up all my claim—I make no pretensions
to any thing in the world; and if I can't get a wife
without fighting for her, by my valour! I'll live a
bachelor.

SIR LUCIUS

Captain, give me your hand: an affront handsomely acknowledged becomes an obligation; and as for the lady, if she chooses to deny her own handwriting, here—— [*Takes out letters.*

MRS. MALAPROP

O, he will dissolve my mystery!—Sir Lucius, perhaps there's some mistake—perhaps I can illuminate——

SIR LUCIUS

Pray, old gentlewoman, don't interfere where you have no business.—Miss Languish, are you my Delia or not?

LYDIA

Indeed, Sir Lucius, I am not.
  [*Walks aside with* CAPTAIN ABSOLUTE.

MRS. MALAPROP

Sir Lucius O'Trigger—ungrateful as you are—I own the soft impeachment—pardon my blushes, I am Delia.

SIR LUCIUS

You Delia—pho! pho! be easy.

MRS. MALAPROP

Why, thou barbarous vandyke—those letters are mine.—When you are more sensible of my benignity —perhaps I may be brought to encourage your addresses.

SIR LUCIUS

Mrs. Malaprop, I am extremely sensible of your con- descension; and whether you or Lucy have put this trick on me, I am equally beholden to you.—And, to show you I am not ungrateful, Captain Absolute, since you have taken that lady from me, I'll give you my Delia into the bargain.

CAPTAIN ABSOLUTE

I am much obliged to you, Sir Lucius; but here's my friend, Fighting Bob, unprovided for.

SIR LUCIUS

Hah! little Valour—here, will you make your fortune?

ACRES

Odds wrinkles! No.—But give me your hand, Sir Lucius, forget and forgive; but if ever I give you a chance of pickling me again, say Bob Acres is a dunce, that's all.

SIR ANTHONY

Come, Mrs. Malaprop, don't be cast down—you are in your bloom yet.

MRS. MALAPROP

O Sir Anthony—men are all barbarians.

[*All retire but* JULIA *and* FAULKLAND.

JULIA

[*Aside.*] He seems dejected and unhappy—not sullen; there was some foundation, however, for the tale he told me—O woman! how true should be your judgment, when your resolution is so weak!

FAULKLAND

Julia!—how can I sue for what I so little deserve? I dare not presume—yet Hope is the child of Penitence.

JULIA

Oh! Faulkland, you have not been more faulty in your unkind treatment of me than I am now in wanting inclination to resent it. As my heart honestly bids me place my weakness to the account of love, I should be ungenerous not to admit the same plea for yours.

FAULKLAND

Now I shall be blest indeed.

SIR ANTHONY

[*Coming forward.*] What's going on here?—So you have been quarrelling too, I warrant? Come, Julia, I never interfered before; but let me have a hand in the matter at last.—All the faults I have ever seen in my friend Faulkland seemed to proceed from what he calls the delicacy and warmth of his affection for you. —There, marry him directly, Julia; you'll find he'll mend surprisingly!

[*The rest come forward.*

SIR LUCIUS

Come, now, I hope there is no dissatisfied person, but what is content; for as I have been disappointed myself, it will be very hard if I have not the satisfaction of seeing other people succeed better.

ACRES

You are right, Sir Lucius.—So, Jack, I wish you joy. —Mr. Faulkland the same.—Ladies,—come now, to show you I'm neither vexed nor angry, odds tabors and pipes! I'll order the fiddles in half an hour to the New Rooms—and I insist on your all meeting me there.

SIR ANTHONY

'Gad! sir, I like your spirit; and at night we single lads will drink a health to the young couples, and a husband to Mrs. Malaprop.

FAULKLAND

Our partners are stolen from us, Jack—I hope to be congratulated by each other—yours for having checked in time the errors of an ill-directed imagination, which might have betrayed an innocent heart; and mine, for having, by her gentleness and candour, reformed the unhappy temper of one, who by it made wretched whom he loved most, and tortured the heart he ought to have adored.

CAPTAIN ABSOLUTE

Well, Jack, we have both tasted the bitters, as well as the sweets of love; with this difference only, that you always prepared the bitter cup for yourself, while I——

LYDIA

Was always obliged to me for it, hey! Mr. Modesty? ——But come, no more of that—our happiness is now as unalloyed as general.

JULIA

Then let us study to preserve it so: and while Hope pictures to us a flattering scene of future bliss, let us deny its pencil those colours which are too bright to be lasting.—When hearts deserving happiness would untie their fortunes, Virtue would crown them with an unfading garland of modest hurtless flowers; but ill-judging Passion will force the gaudier rose into the wreath, whose thorn offends them when its leaves are dropped!   [*Exeunt omnes.*

EPILOGUE

By the Author

SPOKEN BY MRS. BULKLEY

Ladies, for you—I heard our poet say—
He'd try to coax some moral from his play:
'One moral's plain,' cried I, 'without more fuss;
Man's social happiness all rests on us:
Through all the drama—whether damn'd or not—
Love gilds the scene, and women guide the plot.
From every rank obedience is our due—
D'ye doubt?—The world's great stage shall prove it true.'
* The cit, well skill'd to shun domestic strife,*
Will sup abroad; but first he'll ask his wife:
John Trot, his friend, for once will do the same,
But then—he'll just step home to tell his dame.
* The surly squire at noon resolves to rule,*
And half the day—Zounds! madam is a fool!
Convinced at night, the vanquished victor says,
Ah, Kate! you women have such coaxing ways.
* The jolly toper chides each tardy blade,*
Till reeling Bacchus calls on Love for aid:
Then with each toast he sees fair bumpers swim,
And kisses Chloe on the sparkling brim!

Nay, I have heard that statesmen—great and wise—
Will sometimes counsel with a lady's eyes!
The servile suitors watch her various face,
She smiles preferment, or she frowns disgrace,
Curtsies a pension here—there nods a place.

   Nor with less awe, in scenes of humbler life,
Is view'd the mistress, or is heard the wife.
The poorest peasant of the poorest soil,
The child of poverty, and heir to toil,
Early from radiant Love's impartial light
Steals one small spark to cheer this world of night:
Dear spark! that oft through winter's chilling woes
Is all the warmth his little cottage knows!

   The wandering tar, who not for years has press'd,
The widow'd partner of his day of rest,
On the cold deck, far from her arms removed,
Still hums the ditty which his Susan loved;
And while around the cadence rude is blown,
The boatswain whistles in a softer tone.

   The soldier, fairly proud of wounds and toil,
Pants for the triumph of his Nancy's smile!
But ere the battle should he list her cries,
The lover trembles—and the hero dies!
That heart, by war and honour steel'd to fear,
Droops on a sigh, and sickens at a tear!

   But ye more cautious, ye nice-judging few,
Who give to beauty only beauty's due,
Though friends to love—ye view with deep regret
Our conquests marr'd, our triumphs incomplete,

Till polish'd wit more lasting charms disclose,
And judgment fix the darts which beauty throws!
In female breasts did sense and merit rule,
The lover's mind would ask no other school;
Shamed into sense, the scholars of our eyes,
Our beaux from gallantry would soon be wise;
Would gladly light, their homage to improve,
The lamp of knowledge at the torch of love!

THE SCHOOL FOR
SCANDAL
AS PERFORMED
AT THE THEATRE
IN DRURY LANE

CONTENTS

A LIST OF THE PLATES

INTRODUCTION

COMEDY in England has never had a prodigy to equal Chatterton, but it has Congreve and Sheridan as proofs that some very young men may laugh as expertly as others can sigh. Each of these comic poets was only twenty-three when his first play was produced, and neither of them wrote a comedy after thirty. For Sheridan three years were enough. The day he was twenty-six he gave to the stage the farce in which he made fun of bad plays and said good-bye to his own except for some later tinker's work for Drury Lane. With no show of effort, after little experiment, he had already reached in *The School for Scandal* the perfection of artificial comedy. The theatre of his age called for nothing else, and he took his wit off to politics.

He had the advantage that he came towards the end, not the beginning, of a tradition. Though English comedy for a hundred years before Sheridan had bred few dramatists of lasting rank, it had in general been prosperous, disciplined, and skilful. Not touching life too closely or too deeply, it had fixed on certain situations and characters as best suited to the theatre, and had trained actors to represent and audiences to recognize them. It aimed, usually, to mirror a polite society in a polished glass. A playwright who knew the comic stage knew almost all he needed, whatever he might know of the wilderness of passions which is experience.

Sheridan's youth too was an advantage. Years had not taught him to respect the complications of the heart, or even to perceive many of them. What the stage showed him he could accept for the truth of life which it appeared to be. His main outlines were ready-made. Scores of husbands since the Restoration had been worried in comedies over their young wives. Scores of young wives had had their pretty, empty heads turned by the gallants of the town. Scores of gallants had busied themselves with amorous intrigue and schemed for larger inheritances. Scandal, which always has devotees but never has defenders, had been whipped in scores of plays. Sheridan, full of the stage and untroubled by doubt or pity, was free to put all his dashing genius to the invention of fresh incidents and to the manipulation of shining dialogue.

Artificial comedy, one of the most difficult of the forms of literature, makes no demands that a writer of relative inexperience may not meet. Success in the form is a triumph of technique and temper rather than of knowledge or insight.

Sheridan's technique was beyond talent and industry. Much as he might take over directly from the English comic tradition and indirectly from Molière, he had still to bring it to life. While he could have become a connoisseur by study, he could be a virtuoso, at his age, only by genius. It was his genius, with its easy, opulent strength, which, having conceived an academy of tale-bearers, knew how to keep it from being a didactic obstacle in the course of the story. The school in his hands goes through all the paces of scandal, but it flexibly adapts itself to the narrative and helps it along. The whole story moves with the same look of strength. Although the exposition is formal, the action gets speedily under way and thereafter seems to have the momentum of nature as well as the directness of argument. Sheridan never had to learn how to tell a story in the terms of the theatre. The trick was native to him.

With talent and industry he might have thought out two or three striking incidents and then have built up his plot to well-spaced climaxes in them. Genius is more lavish, and Sheridan poured out one happy incident after another. Perhaps the incidents he used were the only ones that occurred to him, but they sound as if they had been chosen from a multitude of inventions of which the play is a brilliant anthology. Perhaps he did not even realize how fine they were. Certainly he did not hover and dawdle over them, as if to catch the last echo of applause. He was swift because he was easy in his art. He was generous because he was rich. He knew by instinct where he was going and what road would be straightest and brightest.

Sheridan's temper was what artificial comedy requires in its writers. Shakespeare, dealing with jealousy, had found Othello agonized and desperate in a tragic passion. Sheridan did not venture so close to experience as that. He could lightly regard it as comic justice that Sir Peter Teazle, having married a young wife, should suffer some of the anxiety he had in his time roused in other husbands. The artificial comedy which would not let Sir Peter be actually cuckolded would not, either, let him win too much sympathy. This was no place for the tempests of real life. Sir Peter must quarrel with Lady Teazle for the entertainment of the spectators, must be jealous, and must in the end be comforted, but he must not endure genuine distress, or at least must not disturbingly reveal it. The young Sheridan lacked the impulse to peer farther and see more. Let comic justice be done.

The young Sheridan, too, could cheerfully take for granted the contrast between Joseph and Charles Surface. Charles was the merry spendthrift, with the heart of gold, that every young man of pleasure likes to think he himself is. Joseph was the sour, sly hypocrite that any young man is guessed by his contemporaries to be when he courts and pleases their elders. Let vice and virtue be exhibited on the stage in lively black and white. In writing artificial comedy, if the best equipment is to know everything about human nature, the next best is not yet to know too much.

What Sheridan needed, and what Sheridan had, was assurance. Writing *The School for Scandal* was playing a game with intricate rules which he must not question. Of course there could never have been so deliberate a coterie of scandalmongers. But, having imagined it, he must, by the rules of this comedy, carry the design as far as logic took him. Of course no Sir Peter and his lady ever went through so much fury with so little hurt, and no two heirs to the same uncle were ever in such symmetrical contrast as Charles and Joseph. But, assuming them for the purposes of his comic game, Sheridan must give them their heads without constantly checking them by reference to the ways of the world outside the game. For the moment the world was narrowed to his stage, and he swayed it laughing.

Besides assurance he had the good nature of high spirits, without contemptuous cynicism. He stood clearly on the side of the amiable if reckless Charles and of the virtuous if priggish Maria. He enjoyed the discomfiture of the snaky Joseph and of the conspiring Lady Sneerwell. High-spirited, he royally enjoyed the entire action of his play and all the persons in it. Even his tale-bearers are tale-makers, creative to the last circumstance. Crabtree, tattling about a duel which has not even taken place, imagines it with a genius's precision: 'Charles's shot took effect, as I tell you, and Sir Peter's missed; but, what is very extraordinary, the ball struck against a little bronze Shakespeare that stood over the fireplace, grazed out of the window at a right angle, and wounded the postman, who was just coming to the door with a double letter from Northamptonshire'. With something of the delight with which these lines must have been put into the mouth of the malicious Crabtree, so soon to be exposed, Sheridan dextrously guided his story through the manœuvres of intrigue. The episodes of the auction and of the screen are the most famous, but there is no let-down after either of them, and the last act, hastily as it is said to have been written, sparkles to the final curtain.

The School for Scandal, brilliantly acted at the first production on 8 May 1777, has had a magnificent history on the stage. It is a play made for actors. The roles are not intricate or profound. The characters are types or caricatures, and the action lends itself to outward expression. But actors to be good in it must have manners and must know how to speak at once formally and nimbly, at once exactly and exuberantly. To muffle the shining dialogue is to shut off half the light the play gives. For Sheridan, no matter what his experience or inexperience, was as much a master of language at twenty-five as if he had been a lyric poet.

In a sense, his comedy should be read or listened to as poetry. These are not such speeches as living men and women now deliver, or ever did. They are human communications wittily essentialized and pointed. When the silly Sir Benjamin Backbite says of his possible future poems that 'a neat rivulet of text shall meander through a meadow of margin', he is, thanks to Sheridan, a comic poet. So with the other speakers. Again and again they say not merely what they are meaning to say, but, thanks to Sheridan, also whatever else the situation has to say for them or about them. They are perfect citizens of artificial comedy, which, although it deals charily with the passions lying below words, is completely articulate about everything within the range of civilized and reasonable minds.   CARL VAN DOREN

A PORTRAIT

ADDRESSED TO MRS. CREWE, WITH THE COMEDY OF THE SCHOOL FOR SCANDAL

By R. B. Sheridan, Esq.

TELL me, ye prime adepts in Scandal's school,
Who rail by precept, and detract by rule,
Lives there no character, so tried, so known,
So deck'd with grace, and so unlike your own,
That even you assist her fame to raise,
Approve by envy, and by silence praise!
Attend!—a model shall attract your view—
Daughters of calumny, I summon you!
You shall decide if this a portrait prove,
Or fond creation of the Muse and Love.
Attend, ye virgin critics, shrewd and sage,
Ye matron censors of this childish age,
Whose peering eye and wrinkled front declare
A fix'd antipathy to young and fair;
By cunning, cautious; or by nature, cold,—
In maiden madness, virulently bold;—
Attend, ye skill'd to coin the precious tale,
Creating proof, where inuendos fail!
Whose practised memories, cruelly exact,
Omit no circumstance, except the fact!—
Attend, all ye who boast,—or old or young,—
The living libel of a slanderous tongue!
So shall my theme, as far contrasted be,
As saints by fiends or hymn by calumny.

Come, gentle Amoret (for 'neath that name
In worthier verse is sung thy beauty's fame),
Come—for but thee who seek the Muse? and while
Celestial blushes check thy conscious smile,
With timid grace and hesitating eye,
The perfect model which I boast supply:—
Vain Muse! couldst thou the humblest sketch create
Of her, or slightest charm couldst imitate—
Could thy blest strain in kindred colours trace
The faintest wonder of her form and face—
Poets would study the immortal line,
And Reynolds own his art subdued by thine;
That art, which well might added lustre give
To nature's best and heaven's superlative:
On Granby's cheek might bid new glories rise,
Or point a purer beam from Devon's eyes!
Hard is the task to shape that beauty's praise,
Whose judgment scorns the homage flattery pays?
But praising Amoret we cannot err,
No tongue o'ervalues Heaven, or flatters her!
Yet she by fate's perverseness—she alone
Would doubt our truth, nor deem such praise her own!
Adorning fashion, unadorn'd by dress,
Simple from taste, and not from carelessness;
Discreet in gesture, in deportment mild,
Not stiff with prudence, nor uncouthly wild:
No state has Amoret; no studied mien;
She frowns no goddess, and she moves no queen,
The softer charm that in her manner lies
Is framed to captivate, yet not surprise;
It justly suits the expression of her face,—
'Tis less than dignity, and more than grace!
On her pure cheek the native hue is such,

That, form'd by Heaven to be admired so much,
The hand divine, with a less partial care,
Might well have fixed a fainter crimson there,
And bade the gentle inmate of her breast—
Inshrined Modesty—supply the rest.
But who the peril of her lips shall paint?
Strip them of smiles—still, still all words are faint!
But moving Love himself appears to teach
Their action, though denied to rule her speech;
And thou who seest her speak, and dost not hear,
Mourn not her distant accents 'scape thine ear;
Viewing those lips, thou still may'st make pretence
To judge of what she says, and swear 'tis sense:
Clothed with such grace, with such expression fraught,
They move in meaning, and they pause in thought!
But dost thou farther watch, with charm'd surprise,
The mild irresolution of her eyes.
Curious to mark how frequent they repose,
In brief eclipse and momentary close—
Ah! seest thou not an ambush'd Cupid there,
Too tim'rous of his charge, with jealous care
Veils and unveils those beams of heavenly light,
Too full, too fatal else, for mortal sight?
Nor yet, such pleasing vengeance fond to meet,
In pard'ning dimples hope a safe retreat.
What though her peaceful breast should ne'er allow
Subduing frowns to arm her altered brow,
By Love, I swear, and by his gentle wiles,
More fatal still the mercy of her smiles!
Thus lovely, thus adorn'd, possessing all
Of bright or fair that can to woman fall,
The height of vanity, might well be thought
Prerogative in her, and Nature's fault.

Yet gentle Amoret, in mind supreme
As well as charms, rejects the vainer theme;
And, half mistrustful of her beauty's store,
She barbs with wit those darts too keen before:—
Read in all knowledge that her sex should reach,
Though Greville, or the Muse, should deign to teach,
Fond to improve, nor timorous to discern
How far it is a woman's grace to learn;
In Millar's dialect she would not prove
Apollo's priestess, but Apollo's love,
Graced by those signs which truth delights to own,
The timid blush, and mild submitted tone:
Whate'er she says, though sense appear throughout,
Displays the tender hue of female doubt;
Deck'd with that charm, how lovely wit appears,
How graceful science, when that robe she wears!
Such too her talents, and her bent of mind,
As speak a sprightly heart by thought refined:
A taste for mirth, by contemplation school'd,
A turn for ridicule, by candour ruled,
A scorn of folly, which she tries to hide;
An awe of talent, which she owns with pride!

   Peace, idle Muse! no more thy strain prolong,
But yield a theme, thy warmest praises wrong;
Just to her merit, though thou canst not raise
Thy feeble verse, behold th' acknowledged praise
Has spread conviction through the envious train,
And cast a fatal gloom o'er Scandal's reign!
And lo! each pallid hag, with blister'd tongue,
Mutters assent to all thy zeal has sung—
Owns all the colours just—the outline true:
Thee my inspirer, and my model—CREWE!

PROLOGUE

WRITTEN BY MR. GARRICK

A SCHOOL for Scandal! tell me, I beseech you,
Needs there a school this modish art to teach you
No need of lessons now, the knowing think;
We might as well be taught to eat and drink.
Caused by a dearth of scandal, should the vapours
Distress our fair ones—let them read the papers;
Their powerful mixtures such disorders hit;
Crave what you will—there's *quantum sufficit*.
'Lord!' cries my Lady Wormwood (who loves tattle,
And puts much salt and pepper in her prattle),
Just risen at noon, all night at cards when threshing
Strong tea and scandal—'Bless me, how refreshing!
Give me the papers, Lisp—how bold and free!   [*Sips.*
Last night Lord L. [Sips] was caught with Lady D.
For aching heads what charming sal volatile!   [*Sips.*
If Mrs. B. will still continue flirting,
We hope she'll DRAW, *or we'll* UNDRAW *the curtain.*
Fine satire, poz—in public all abuse it,
But, by ourselves [*Sips*], our praise we can't refuse it.
Now, Lisp, read you—there, at that dash and star.'
'Yes, ma'am—*A certain Lord had best beware,*
Who lives not twenty miles from Grosvenor Square;
For should he Lady W. find willing,
Wormwood is bitter'—'Oh! that's me! the villain!

173

Throw it behind the fire, and never more
Let that vile paper come within my door.'
Thus at our friends we laugh, who feel the dart;
To reach our feelings, we ourselves must smart.
Is our young bard so young, to think that he
Can stop the full spring-tide of calumny?
Knows he the world so little, and its trade?
Alas! the devil's sooner raised than laid.
So strong, so swift, the monster there's no gagging:
Cut Scandal's head off, still the tongue is wagging.
Proud of your smiles once lavishly bestow'd,
Again our young Don Quixote takes the road;
To show his gratitude he draws his pen,
And seeks his hydra, Scandal, in his den.
For your applause all perils he would through—
He'll fight—that's write—a cavalliero true,
Till every drop of blood—that's ink—is spilt for you.

DRAMATIS PERSONÆ

AS ORIGINALLY ACTED AT DRURY LANE
THEATRE IN 1777

———

SIR PETER TEAZLE	*Mr. King*
SIR OLIVER SURFACE	*Mr. Yates*
SIR HARRY BUMPER	*Mr. Gawdry*
SIR BENJAMIN BACKBITE	*Mr. Dodd*
JOSEPH SURFACE	*Mr. Palmer*
CHARLES SURFACE	*Mr. Smith*
CARELESS	*Mr. Farren*
SNAKE	*Mr. Packer*
CRABTREE	*Mr. Parsons*
ROWLEY	*Mr. Aickin*
MOSES	*Mr. Baddeley*
TRIP	*Mr. Lamash*
LADY TEAZLE	*Mrs. Abington*
LADY SNEERWELL	*Miss Sherry*
MRS. CANDOUR	*Miss Pope*
MARIA	*Miss P. Hopkins*

Gentlemen, Maid, *and* Servants

SCENE: LONDON

ACT ONE

SCENE ONE

LADY SNEERWELL'S *Dressing-room*

LADY SNEERWELL *discovered at her toilet;*

SNAKE *drinking chocolate*

LADY SNEERWELL

The paragraphs, you say, Mr. Snake, were all inserted?

SNAKE

They were, madam; and, as I copied them myself in a feigned hand, there can be no suspicion whence they came.

LADY SNEERWELL

Did you circulate the report of Lady Brittle's intrigue with Captain Boastall?

SNAKE

That's in as fine a train as your ladyship could wish. In the common course of things, I think it must reach Mrs. Clackitt's ears within four-and-twenty hours; and then, you know, the business is as good as done.

LADY SNEERWELL

Why, truly, Mrs. Clackitt has a very pretty talent, and a great deal of industry.

SNAKE

True, madam, and has been tolerably successful in her day. To my knowledge, she has been the cause of six matches being broken off, and three sons being disinherited; of four forced elopements, and as many close confinements; nine separate maintenances, and two divorces. Nay, I have more than once traced her causing a *tête-à-tête* in the *Town and Country Magazine*, when the parties, perhaps, had never seen each other's face before in the course of their lives.

LADY SNEERWELL

She certainly has talents, but her manner is gross.

SNAKE

'Tis very true. She generally designs well, has a free tongue and a bold invention; but her colouring is too dark, and her outlines often extravagant. She wants that delicacy of tint, and mellowness of sneer, which distinguish your ladyship's scandal.

LADY SNEERWELL

You are partial, Snake.

SNAKE

Not in the least; everybody allows that Lady Sneerwell can do more with a word or look than many can with the most laboured detail, even when they happen to have a little truth on their side to support it.

LADY SNEERWELL

Yes, my dear Snake; and I am no hypocrite to deny the satisfaction I reap from the success of my efforts. Wounded myself, in the early part of my life, by the envenomed tongue of slander, I confess I have since known no pleasure equal to the reducing others to the level of my own injured reputation.

SNAKE

Nothing can be more natural. But, Lady Sneerwell, there is one affair in which you have lately employed me, wherein, I confess, I am at a loss to guess your motives.

LADY SNEERWELL

I conceive you mean with respect to my neighbour, Sir Peter Teazle, and his family?

SNAKE

I do. Here are two young men, to whom Sir Peter has acted as a kind of guardian since their father's death; the eldest possessing the most amiable character, and universally well spoken of—the youngest, the most dissipated and extravagant young fellow in the kingdom, without friends or character: the former an avowed admirer of your ladyship, and apparently your favourite; the latter attached to Maria, Sir Peter's ward, and confessedly beloved by her. Now, on the face of these circumstances, it is utterly unaccountable to me, why you, the widow of a city knight, with a good jointure, should not close with the passion of a man of such character and expectations as Mr. Surface; and more so why you should be so uncommonly earnest to destroy the mutual attachment subsisting between his brother Charles and Maria.

LADY SNEERWELL

Then, at once to unravel this mystery, I must inform you that love has no share whatever in the intercourse between Mr. Surface and me.

SNAKE

No!

LADY SNEERWELL

His real attachment is to Maria or her fortune; but, finding in his brother a favoured rival, he has been obliged to mask his pretensions, and profit by my assistance.

SNAKE

Yet still I am more puzzled why you should interest yourself in his success.

LADY SNEERWELL

Heavens! how dull you are! Cannot you surmise the weakness which I hitherto, through shame, have concealed even from you? Must I confess that Charles—that libertine, that extravagant, that bankrupt in fortune and reputation—that he it is for whom I am thus anxious and malicious, and to gain whom I would sacrifice everything?

SNAKE

Now, indeed, your conduct appears consistent; but how came you and Mr. Surface so confidential?

LADY SNEERWELL

For our mutual interest. I have found him out a long time since. I know him to be artful, selfish, and malicious—in short, a sentimental knave; while with Sir Peter, and indeed with all his acquaintance, he passes for a youthful miracle of prudence, good sense, and benevolence.

SNAKE

Yes; yet Sir Peter vows he has not his equal in England; and, above all, he praises him as a man of sentiment.

LADY SNEERWELL

True; and with the assistance of his sentiment and hypocrisy he has brought Sir Peter entirely into his interest with regard to Maria; while poor Charles has no friend in the house—though, I fear, he has a powerful one in Maria's heart, against whom we must direct our schemes.

Enter SERVANT

SERVANT

Mr. Surface.

LADY SNEERWELL

Show him up.—[*Exit* SERVANT.] He generally calls about this time. I don't wonder at people giving him to me for a lover.

Enter JOSEPH SURFACE

JOSEPH SURFACE

My dear Lady Sneerwell, how do you do to-day? Mr. Snake, your most obedient.

LADY SNEERWELL

Snake has just been rallying me on our mutual attachment; but I have informed him of our real views. You know how useful he has been to us; and, believe me, the confidence is not ill-placed.

JOSEPH SURFACE

Madam, it is impossible for me to suspect a man of Mr. Snake's sensibility and discernment.

LADY SNEERWELL

Well, well, no compliments now; but tell me when you saw your mistress, Maria—or, what is more material to me, your brother.

JOSEPH SURFACE

I have not seen either since I left you; but I can inform you that they never meet. Some of your stories have taken a good effect on Maria.

LADY SNEERWELL

Ah, my dear Snake! the merit of this belongs to you. But do your brother's distresses increase?

JOSEPH SURFACE

Every hour. I am told he has had another execution in the house yesterday. In short, his dissipation and extravagance exceed anything I have ever heard of.

LADY SNEERWELL

Poor Charles!

JOSEPH SURFACE

True, madam; notwithstanding his vices, one can't help feeling for him. Poor Charles! I'm sure I wish it were in my power to be of any essential service to him; for the man who does not share in the distresses of a brother, even though merited by his own misconduct, deserves——

LADY SNEERWELL

O Lud! you are going to be moral, and forget that you are among friends.

JOSEPH SURFACE

Egad, that's true! I'll keep that sentiment till I see Sir Peter. However, it is certainly a charity to rescue Maria from such a libertine, who, if he is to be reclaimed, can be so only by a person of your lady-ship's superior accomplishments and understanding.

SNAKE

I believe, Lady Sneerwell, here's company coming: I'll go and copy the letter I mentioned to you. Mr. Surface, your most obedient.

JOSEPH SURFACE

Sir, your very devoted.—[*Exit* SNAKE.] Lady Sneerwell, I am very sorry you have put any farther confidence in that fellow.

LADY SNEERWELL

Why so?

JOSEPH SURFACE

I have lately detected him in frequent conference with old Rowley, who was formerly my father's steward, and has never, you know, been a friend of mine.

LADY SNEERWELL

And do you think he would betray us?

JOSEPH SURFACE

Nothing more likely: take my word for't, Lady Sneerwell, that fellow hasn't virtue enough to be faithful even to his own villany. Ah, Maria!

Enter MARIA

LADY SNEERWELL

Maria, my dear, how do you do? What's the matter?

MARIA

Oh! there's that disagreeable lover of mine, Sir Benjamin Backbite, has just called at my guardian's, with his odious uncle, Crabtree; so I slipped out, and ran hither to avoid them.

LADY SNEERWELL

Is that all?

JOSEPH SURFACE

If my brother Charles had been of the party, madam, perhaps you would not have been so much alarmed.

LADY SNEERWELL

Nay, now you are severe; for I dare swear the truth of the matter is, Maria heard you were here. But, my dear, what has Sir Benjamin done, that you should avoid him so?

MARIA

Oh, he has done nothing—but 'tis for what he has said: his conversation is a perpetual libel on all his acquaintance.

JOSEPH SURFACE

Ay, and the worst of it is, there is no advantage in not knowing him; for he'll abuse a stranger just as soon as his best friend: and his uncle's as bad.

LADY SNEERWELL

Nay, but we should make allowance; Sir Benjamin is a wit and a poet.

MARIA

For my part, I own, madam, wit loses its respect with me, when I see it in company with malice. What do you think, Mr. Surface?

JOSEPH SURFACE

Certainly, madam; to smile at the jest which plants a thorn in another's breast is to become a principal in the mischief.

LADY SNEERWELL

Psha! there's no possibility of being witty without a little ill-nature: the malice of a good thing is the barb that makes it stick. What's your opinion, Mr. Surface?

LADY SNEERWELL

JOSEPH SURFACE

To be sure, madam; that conversation, where the spirit of raillery is suppressed, will ever appear tedious and insipid.

MARIA

Well, I'll not debate how far scandal may be allowable; but in a man, I am sure, it is always contemptible. We have pride, envy, rivalship, and a thousand motives to depreciate each other; but the male slanderer must have the cowardice of a woman before he can traduce one.

Re-enter SERVANT

SERVANT

Madam, Mrs. Candour is below, and, if your ladyship's at leisure, will leave her carriage.

LADY SNEERWELL

Beg her to walk in.—[*Exit* SERVANT.] Now, Maria, here is a character to your taste; for, though Mrs. Candour is a little talkative, everybody knows her to be the best-natured and best sort of woman.

MARIA

Yes, with a very gross affectation of good nature and benevolence, she does more mischief than the direct malice of old Crabtree.

JOSEPH SURFACE

I'faith that's true, Lady Sneerwell: whenever I hear the current running against the characters of my friends, I never think them in such danger as when Candour undertakes their defence.

LADY SNEERWELL
Hush!—here she is!

Enter MRS. CANDOUR

MRS. CANDOUR
My dear Lady Sneerwell, how have you been this century?—Mr. Surface, what news do you hear?—though indeed it is no matter, for I think one hears nothing else but scandal.

JOSEPH SURFACE
Just so, indeed, ma'am.

MRS. CANDOUR
Oh, Maria! child,—what, is the whole affair off between you and Charles? His extravagance, I presume—the town talks of nothing else.

MARIA
I am very sorry, ma'am, the town has so little to do.

MRS. CANDOUR
True, true, child: but there's no stopping people's tongues. I own I was hurt to hear it, as I indeed was to learn, from the same quarter, that your guardian, Sir Peter, and Lady Teazle have not agreed lately as well as could be wished.

MARIA
'Tis strangely impertinent for people to busy themselves so.

MRS. CANDOUR
Very true, child; but what's to be done? People will talk—there's no preventing it. Why, it was but yesterday I was told that Miss Gadabout had eloped with Sir Filagree Flirt. But, Lord! there's no minding

what one hears; though, to be sure, I had this from very good authority.

MARIA

Such reports are highly scandalous.

MRS. CANDOUR

So they are, child—shameful, shameful! But the world is so censorious, no character escapes. Lord, now who would have suspected your friend, Miss Prim, of an indiscretion? Yet such is the ill-nature of people, that they say her uncle stopped her last week, just as she was stepping into the York mail with her dancing-master.

MARIA

I'll answer for't there are no grounds for that report.

MRS. CANDOUR

Ah, no foundation in the world, I dare swear: no more, probably, than for the story circulated last month, of Mrs. Festino's affair with Colonel Cassino —though, to be sure, that matter was never rightly cleared up.

JOSEPH SURFACE

The license of invention some people take is monstrous indeed.

MARIA

'Tis so; but, in my opinion, those who report such things are equally culpable.

MRS. CANDOUR

To be sure they are; tale-bearers are as bad as the tale-makers—'tis an old observation, and a very true one: but what's to be done, as I said before? how will you prevent people from talking? To-day, Mrs.

Clackitt assured me, Mr. and Mrs. Honeymoon were at last become mere man and wife, like the rest of their acquaintance. She likewise hinted that a certain widow, in the next street, had got rid of her dropsy and recovered her shape in a most surprising manner. And at the same time Miss Tattle, who was by, affirmed, that Lord Buffalo had discovered his lady at a house of no extraordinary fame; and that Sir Harry Bouquet and Tom Saunter were to measure swords on a similar provocation. But, Lord, do you think I would report these things! No, no! tale-bearers, as I said before, are just as bad as the tale-makers.

JOSEPH SURFACE

Ah! Mrs. Candour, if everybody had your forbearance and good nature!

MRS. CANDOUR

I confess, Mr. Surface, I cannot bear to hear people attacked behind their backs; and when ugly circumstances come out against our acquaintance I own I always love to think the best. By-the-by, I hope 'tis not true that your brother is absolutely ruined?

JOSEPH SURFACE

I am afraid his circumstances are very bad indeed, ma'am.

MRS. CANDOUR

Ah!—I heard so—but you must tell him to keep up his spirits; everybody almost is in the same way: Lord Spindle, Sir Thomas Splint, Captain Quinze, and Mr. Nickit—all up, I hear, within this week; so, if Charles is undone, he'll find half his acquaintance ruined too, and that, you know, is a consolation.

JOSEPH SURFACE
Doubtless, ma'am—a very great one.

Re-enter SERVANT

SERVANT
Mr. Crabtree and Sir Benjamin Backbite.   [*Exit.*

LADY SNEERWELL
So, Maria, you see your lover pursues you; positively you shan't escape.

Enter CRABTREE *and*

SIR BENJAMIN BACKBITE

CRABTREE
Lady Sneerwell, I kiss your hand. Mrs. Candour, I don't believe you are acquainted with my nephew, Sir Benjamin Backbite? Egad, ma'am, he has a pretty wit, and is a pretty poet too. Isn't he, Lady Sneerwell?

SIR BENJAMIN
Oh, fie, uncle!

CRABTREE
Nay, egad it's true: I back him at a rebus or a charade against the best rhymer in the kingdom. Has your ladyship heard the epigram he wrote last week on Lady Frizzle's feather catching fire?—Do, Benjamin, repeat it, or the charade you made last night extempore at Mrs. Drowzie's conversazione. Come now; your first is the name of a fish, your second a great naval commander, and——

SIR BENJAMIN
Uncle, now—pr'ythee——

CRABTREE

I'faith, ma'am, 'twould surprise you to hear how ready he is at all these sort of things.

LADY SNEERWELL

I wonder, Sir Benjamin, you never publish anything.

SIR BENJAMIN

To say truth, ma'am, 'tis very vulgar to print; and, as my little productions are mostly satires and lampoons on particular people, I find they circulate more by giving copies in confidence to the friends of the parties. However, I have some love elegies, which, when favoured with this lady's smiles, I mean to give the public.   [*Pointing to* MARIA.

CRABTREE

[*To* MARIA.] 'Fore heaven, ma'am, they'll immortalize you!—you will be handed down to posterity, like Petrarch's Laura, or Waller's Sacharissa.

SIR BENJAMIN

[*To* MARIA.] Yes, madam, I think you will like them, when you shall see them on a beautiful quarto page, where a neat rivulet of text shall meander through a meadow of margin. 'Fore Gad, they will be the most elegant things of their kind!

CRABTREE

But, ladies, that's true—have you heard the news?

MRS. CANDOUR

What, sir, do you mean the report of—

CRABTREE

No, ma'am, that's not it.—Miss Nicely is going to be married to her own footman.

MRS. CANDOUR

Impossible!

CRABTREE

Ask Sir Benjamin.

SIR BENJAMIN

'Tis very true, ma'am: everything is fixed, and the wedding liveries bespoke.

CRABTREE

Yes—and they do say there were pressing reasons for it.

LADY SNEERWELL

Why, I have heard something of this before.

MRS. CANDOUR

It can't be—and I wonder any one should believe such a story of so prudent a lady as Miss Nicely.

SIR BENJAMIN

O Lud! ma'am, that's the very reason 'twas believed at once. She has always been so cautious and so reserved, that everybody was sure there was some reason for it at bottom.

MRS. CANDOUR

Why, to be sure, a tale of scandal is as fatal to the credit of a prudent lady of her stamp as a fever is generally to those of the strongest constitutions. But there is a sort of puny sickly reputation, that is always ailing, yet will outlive the robuster characters of a hundred prudes.

SIR BENJAMIN

True, madam, there are valetudinarians in reputation as well as constitution, who, being conscious of their weak part, avoid the least breath of air, and supply their want of stamina by care and circumspection.

MRS. CANDOUR

Well, but this may be all a mistake. You know, Sir Benjamin, very trifling circumstances often give rise to the most injurious tales.

CRABTREE

That they do, I'll be sworn, ma'am. Did you ever hear how Miss Piper came to lose her lover and her character last summer at Tunbridge?—Sir Benjamin, you remember it?

SIR BENJAMIN

Oh, to be sure!—the most whimsical circumstance.

LADY SNEERWELL

How was it, pray?

CRABTREE

Why, one evening, at Mrs. Ponto's assembly, the conversation happened to turn on the breeding Nova Scotia sheep in this country. Says a young lady in company, I have known instances of it; for Miss Letitia Piper, a first cousin of mine, had a Nova Scotia sheep that produced her twins. 'What!' cries the Lady Dowager Dundizzy (who you know is as deaf as a post), 'has Miss Piper had twins?' This mistake, as you may imagine, threw the whole company into a fit of laughter. However, 'twas the next morning everywhere reported, and in a few days believed by the whole town, that Miss Letitia Piper had actually been brought to bed of a fine boy and girl: and in less than a week there were some people who could name the father, and the farm-house where the babies were put to nurse.

Mrs. CANDOUR.

MRS. CANDOUR

LADY SNEERWELL
Strange, indeed!

CRABTREE
Matter of fact, I assure you. O Lud! Mr. Surface, pray is it true that your uncle, Sir Oliver, is coming home?

JOSEPH SURFACE
Not that I know of, indeed, sir.

CRABTREE
He has been in the East Indies a long time. You can scarcely remember him, I believe? Sad comfort, whenever he returns, to hear how your brother has gone on!

JOSEPH SURFACE
Charles has been imprudent, sir, to be sure; but I hope no busy people have already prejudiced Sir Oliver against him. He may reform.

SIR BENJAMIN
To be sure he may; for my part I never believed him to be so utterly void of principle as people say; and though he has lost all his friends, I am told nobody is better spoken of by the Jews.

CRABTREE
That's true, egad, nephew. If the old Jewry was a ward, I believe Charles would be an alderman: no man more popular there, 'fore Gad! I hear he pays as many annuities as the Irish tontine; and that, whenever he is sick, they have prayers for the recovery of his health in all the synagogues.

SIR BENJAMIN

Yet no man lives in greater splendour. They tell me, when he entertains his friends he will sit down to dinner with a dozen of his own securities; have a score of tradesmen in the antechamber, and an officer behind every guest's chair.

JOSEPH SURFACE

This may be entertainment to you, gentlemen, but you pay very little regard to the feelings of a brother.

MARIA

[*Aside*.] Their malice is intolerable!—[*Aloud*.] Lady Sneerwell, I must wish you a good morning: I'm not very well. [*Exit.*

MRS. CANDOUR

O dear! she changes colour very much.

LADY SNEERWELL

Do, Mrs. Candour, follow her; she may want your assistance.

MRS. CANDOUR

That I will, with all my soul, ma'am.—Poor dear girl, who knows what her situation may be! [*Exit.*

LADY SNEERWELL

'Twas nothing but that she could not bear to hear Charles reflected on, notwithstanding their difference.

SIR BENJAMIN

The young lady's *penchant* is obvious.

CRABTREE

But, Benjamin, you must not give up the pursuit for that: follow her, and put her into good humour. Repeat her some of your own verses. Come, I'll assist you.

SIR BENJAMIN

Mr. Surface, I did not mean to hurt you; but depend on't your brother is utterly undone.

CRABTREE

O Lud, ay! undone as ever man was—can't raise a guinea.

SIR BENJAMIN

And everything sold, I'm told, that was movable.

CRABTREE

I have seen one that was at his house. Not a thing left but some empty bottles that were overlooked, and the family pictures, which I believe are framed in the wainscots.

SIR BENJAMIN

And I'm very sorry also to hear some bad stories against him. [*Going.*

CRABTREE

Oh, he has done many mean things, that's certain.

SIR BENJAMIN

But, however, as he's your brother—— [*Going.*

CRABTREE

We'll tell you all another opportunity.

[*Exeunt* CRABTREE *and* SIR BENJAMIN.

LADY SNEERWELL

Ha, ha! 'tis very hard for them to leave a subject they have not quite run down.

JOSEPH SURFACE

And I believe the abuse was no more acceptable to your ladyship than to Maria.

LADY SNEERWELL

I doubt her affections are further engaged than we imagine. But the family are to be here this evening, so you may as well dine where you are, and we shall have an opportunity of observing further; in the meantime, I'll go and plot mischief, and you shall study sentiment.   [*Exeunt.*

SCENE TWO

A Room in SIR PETER TEAZLE'S *House*

Enter SIR PETER TEAZLE

SIR PETER

When an old bachelor marries a young wife, what is he to expect? 'Tis now six months since Lady Teazle made me the happiest of men—and I have been the most miserable dog ever since! We tift a little going to church, and fairly quarrelled before the bells had done ringing. I was more than once nearly choked with gall during the honeymoon, and had lost all comfort in life before my friends had done wishing me joy. Yet I chose with caution—a girl bred wholly in the country, who never knew luxury beyond one silk gown, nor dissipation above the annual gala of a race ball. Yet she now plays her part in all the extravagant fopperies of fashion and the town, with as ready a grace as if she never had seen a bush or a grass-plot out of Grosvenor Square! I am sneered at by all my acquaintance, and paragraphed in the newspapers. She dissipates my fortune, and contradicts all my humours; yet the worst of it is, I doubt I love her, or

I should never bear all this. However, I'll never be weak enough to own it.

Enter ROWLEY

ROWLEY

Oh! Sir Peter, your servant: how is it with you, sir?

SIR PETER

Very bad, Master Rowley, very bad. I meet with nothing but crosses and vexations.

ROWLEY

What can have happened since yesterday?

SIR PETER

A good question to a married man!

ROWLEY

Nay, I'm sure, Sir Peter, your lady can't be the cause of your uneasiness.

SIR PETER

Why, has anybody told you she was dead?

ROWLEY

Come, come, Sir Peter, you love her, notwithstanding your tempers don't exactly agree.

SIR PETER

But the fault is entirely hers, Master Rowley. I am, myself, the sweetest-tempered man alive, and hate a teasing temper; and so I tell her a hundred times a day.

ROWLEY

Indeed!

SIR PETER

Ay; and what is very extraordinary, in all our disputes she is always in the wrong! But Lady Sneerwell, and and the set she meets at her house, encourage the perverseness of her disposition. Then, to complete my vexation, Maria, my ward, whom I ought to have the power of a father over, is determined to turn rebel too, and absolutely refuses the man whom I have long resolved on for her husband; meaning, I suppose, to bestow herself on his profligate brother.

ROWLEY

You know, Sir Peter, I have always taken the liberty to differ with you on the subject of these two young gentlemen. I only wish you may not be deceived in your opinion of the elder. For Charles, my life on't! he will retrieve his errors yet. Their worthy father, once my honoured master, was, at his years, nearly as wild a spark; yet, when he died, he did not leave a more benevolent heart to lament his loss.

SIR PETER

You are wrong, Master Rowley. On their father's death, you know, I acted as a kind of guardian to them both, till their uncle Sir Oliver's liberality gave them an early independence: of course, no person could have more opportunities of judging of their hearts, and I was never mistaken in my life. Joseph is indeed a model for the young men of the age. He is a man of sentiment, and acts up to the sentiments he professes; but, for the other, take my word for't, if he had any grain of virtue by descent, he has dissipated it with the rest of his inheritance. Ah! my old friend, Sir

Oliver, will be deeply mortified when he finds how part of his bounty has been misapplied.

ROWLEY

I am sorry to find you so violent against the young man, because this may be the most critical period of his fortune. I came hither with news that will surprise you.

SIR PETER

What! let me hear.

ROWLEY

Sir Oliver is arrived, and at this moment in town.

SIR PETER

How! you astonish me! I thought you did not expect him this month.

ROWLEY

I did not: but his passage has been remarkably quick.

SIR PETER

Egad, I shall rejoice to see my old friend. 'Tis sixteen years since we met. We have had many a day together: but does he still enjoin us not to inform his nephews of his arrival?

ROWLEY

Most strictly. He means, before it is known, to make some trial of their dispositions.

SIR PETER

Ah! There needs no art to discover their merits— however, he shall have his way; but, pray, does he know I am married?

ROWLEY

Yes, and will soon wish you joy.

SIR PETER

What, as we drink health to a friend in consumption!
Ah, Oliver will laugh at me. We used to rail at matri-
mony together, but he has been steady to his text.
Well, he must be soon at my house, though—I'll
instantly give orders for his reception. But, Master
Rowley, don't drop a word that Lady Teazle and
I ever disagree.

ROWLEY

By no means.

SIR PETER

For I should never be able to stand Noll's jokes; so
I'll have him think, Lord forgive me! that we are a
very happy couple.

ROWLEY

I understand you:—but then you must be very careful not to differ while he is in the house with you.

SIR PETER

Egad, and so we must—and that's impossible. Ah!
Master Rowley, when an old bachelor marries a
young wife, he deserves—no—the crime carries its
punishment along with it.   [*Exeunt.*

ACT TWO

SCENE ONE

A Room in SIR PETER TEAZLE'S *House*

Enter SIR PETER *and* LADY TEAZLE

SIR PETER

Lady Teazle, Lady Teazle, I'll not bear it!

LADY TEAZLE

Sir Peter, Sir Peter, you may bear it or not, as you please; but I ought to have my own way in everything, and what's more, I will too. What though I was educated in the country, I know very well that women of fashion in London are accountable to nobody after they are married.

SIR PETER

Very well, ma'am, very well; so a husband is to have no influence, no authority?

LADY TEAZLE

Authority! No, to be sure:—if you wanted authority over me, you should have adopted me, and not married me: I am sure you were old enough.

SIR PETER

Old enough!—ay, there it is! Well, well, Lady Teazle, although my life may be made unhappy by your temper, I'll not be ruined by your extravagance!

LADY TEAZLE

My extravagance! I'm sure I'm not more extravagant than a woman of fashion ought to be.

SIR PETER

No, no, madam, you shall throw away no more sums on such unmeaning luxury. 'Slife! to spend as much to furnish your dressing-room with flowers in winter as would suffice to turn the Pantheon into a greenhouse, and give a *fête champêtre* at Christmas.

LADY TEAZLE

And am I to blame, Sir Peter, because flowers are dear in cold weather? You should find fault with the climate, and not with me. For my part, I'm sure I wish it was spring all the year round, and that roses grew under our feet!

SIR PETER

Oons! madam—if you had been born to this, I shouldn't wonder at your talking thus; but you forget what your situation was when I married you.

LADY TEAZLE

No, no, I don't; 'twas a very disagreeable one, or I should never have married you.

SIR PETER

Yes, yes, madam, you were then in somewhat a humbler style—the daughter of a plain country squire. Recollect, Lady Teazle, when I saw you first sitting at your tambour, in a pretty figured linen gown, with a bunch of keys at your side, your hair combed smooth over a roll, and your apartment hung round with fruits in worsted, of your own working.

LADY TEAZLE

Oh, yes! I remember it very well, and a curious life I led. My daily occupation to inspect the dairy, superintend the poultry, make extracts from the family receipt-book, and comb my aunt Deborah's lapdog.

SIR PETER

Yes, yes, ma'am, 'twas so indeed.

LADY TEAZLE

And then, you know, my evening amusements! To draw patterns for ruffles, which I had not the materials to make up; to play Pope Joan with the Curate; to read a sermon to my aunt; or to be stuck down to an old spinet to strum my father to sleep after a fox-chase.

SIR PETER

I am glad you have so good a memory. Yes, madam, these were the recreations I took you from; but now you must have your coach—*vis-à-vis*—and three powdered footmen before your chair; and, in the summer, a pair of white cats to draw you to Kensington Gardens. No recollection, I suppose, when you were content to ride double, behind the butler, on a docked coach-horse?

LADY TEAZLE

No—I swear I never did that; I deny the butler and the coach-horse.

SIR PETER

This, madam, was your situation; and what have I done for you? I have made you a woman of fashion, of fortune, of rank—in short, I have made you my wife.

LADY TEAZLE

Well, then, and there is but one thing more you can make me to add to the obligation, that is——

SIR PETER

My widow, I suppose?

LADY TEAZLE

Hem! hem!

SIR PETER

I thank you, madam—but don't flatter yourself; for, though your ill-conduct may disturb my peace of mind, it shall never break my heart, I promise you: however, I am equally obliged to you for the hint.

LADY TEAZLE

Then why will you endeavour to make yourself so disagreeable to me, and thwart me in every little elegant expense?

SIR PETER

'Slife, madam, I say, had you any of these little elegant expenses when you married me?

LADY TEAZLE

Lud, Sir Peter! would you have me be out of the fashion?

SIR PETER

The fashion, indeed! what had you to do with the fashion before you married me?

LADY TEAZLE

For my part, I should think you would like to have your wife thought a woman of taste.

SIR PETER

Ay—there again—taste! Zounds! madam, you had no taste when you married me!

LADY TEAZLE

That's very true, indeed, Sir Peter! and, after having married you, I should never pretend to taste again, I allow. But now, Sir Peter, since we have finished our daily jangle, I presume I may go to my engagement at Lady Sneerwell's?

SIR PETER

Ay, there's another precious circumstance—a charming set of acquaintance you have made there!

LADY TEAZLE

Nay, Sir Peter, they are all people of rank and fortune, and remarkably tenacious of reputation.

SIR PETER

Yes, egad, they are tenacious of reputation with a vengeance; for they don't choose anybody should have a character but themselves! Such a crew! Ah! many a wretch has rid on a hurdle who has done less mischief than these utterers of forged tales, coiners of scandal, and clippers of reputation.

LADY TEAZLE

What, would you restrain the freedom of speech?

SIR PETER

Ah! they have made you just as bad as any one of the society.

LADY TEAZLE

Why, I believe I do bear a part with a tolerable grace. But I vow I bear no malice against the people I abuse: when I say an ill-natured thing, 'tis out of pure good humour; and I take it for granted they deal exactly in the same manner with me. But, Sir Peter, you know you promised to come to Lady Sneerwell's too.

SIR PETER

Well, well, I'll call in just to look after my own character.

LADY TEAZLE

Then, indeed, you must make haste after me or you'll be too late. So good-bye to ye.   [*Exit.*

SIR PETER

So—I have gained much by my intended expostulation! Yet with what a charming air she contradicts everything I say, and how pleasantly she shows her contempt for my authority! Well, though I can't make her love me, there is great satisfaction in quarrelling with her; and I think she never appears to such advantage as when she is doing everything in her power to plague me.   [*Exit.*

SCENE TWO

A Room in LADY SNEERWELL'S *House*

LADY SNEERWELL, MRS. CANDOUR, CRABTREE, SIR BENJAMIN BACKBITE, *and* JOSEPH SURFACE, *discovered*

LADY SNEERWELL

Nay, positively, we will hear it.

JOSEPH SURFACE

Yes, yes, the epigram, by all means.

SIR BENJAMIN

O plague on't, uncle! 'tis mere nonsense.

CRABTREE

No, no; 'fore Gad, very clever for an extempore!

SIR BENJAMIN

But, ladies, you should be acquainted with the circumstance. You must know, that one day last week,
as Lady Betty Curricle was taking the dust in Hyde
Park, in a sort of duodecimo phaeton, she desired me
to write some verses on her ponies; upon which, I
took out my pocket-book, and in one moment
produced the following:

Sure never were seen two such beautiful ponies;
Other horses are clowns, but these macaronies:
To give them this title I am sure can't be wrong.
Their legs are so slim, and their tails are so long.

CRABTREE

There, ladies, done in the smack of a whip, and on
horseback too.

JOSEPH SURFACE

A very Phœbus, mounted—indeed, Sir Benjamin!

SIR BENJAMIN

Oh dear, sir!—trifles—trifles.—

Enter LADY TEAZLE *and* MARIA

MRS. CANDOUR

I must have a copy.

LADY SNEERWELL

Lady Teazle, I hope we shall see Sir Peter?

LADY TEAZLE

I believe he'll wait on your ladyship presently.

LADY SNEERWELL

Maria, my love, you look grave. Come, you shall sit
down to piquet with Mr. Surface.

MARIA

I take very little pleasure in cards—however, I'll do as your ladyship pleases.

LADY TEAZLE

I am surprised Mr. Surface should sit down with her; I thought he would have embraced this opportunity of speaking to me before Sir Peter came.   [*Aside.*

MRS. CANDOUR

Now, I'll die; but you are so scandalous, I'll forswear your society.

LADY TEAZLE

What's the matter, Mrs. Candour?

MRS. CANDOUR

They'll not allow our friend Miss Vermillion to be handsome.

LADY SNEERWELL

Oh, surely she is a pretty woman.

CRABTREE

I am very glad you think so, ma'am.

MRS. CANDOUR

She has a charming fresh colour.

LADY TEAZLE

Yes, when it is fresh put on.

MRS. CANDOUR

Oh, fie! I'll swear her colour is natural: I have seen it come and go!

LADY TEAZLE

I dare swear you have, ma'am: it goes off at night, and comes again in the morning.

LADY TEAZLE

SIR BENJAMIN

True, ma'am, it not only comes and goes; but, what's more, egad, her maid can fetch and carry it!

MRS. CANDOUR

Ha! ha! ha! how I hate to hear you talk so! But surely, now, her sister is, or was, very handsome.

CRABTREE

Who? Mrs. Evergreen? O Lord! she's six-and-fifty if she's an hour!

MRS. CANDOUR

Now positively you wrong her; fifty-two or fifty-three is the utmost—and I don't think she looks more.

SIR BENJAMIN

Ah! there's no judging by her looks, unless one could see her face.

LADY SNEERWELL

Well, well, if Mrs. Evergreen does take some pains to repair the ravages of time, you must allow she effects it with great ingenuity; and surely that's better than the careless manner in which the widow Ochre caulks her wrinkles.

SIR BENJAMIN

Nay, now, Lady Sneerwell, you are severe upon the widow. Come, come, 'tis not that she paints so ill— but, when she has finished her face, she joins it on so badly to her neck, that she looks like a mended statue, in which the connoisseur may see at once that the head's modern, though the trunk's antique!

CRABTREE

Ha! ha! ha! Well said, nephew!

MRS. CANDOUR

Ha! ha! ha! Well, you make me laugh; but I vow I hate you for it. What do you think of Miss Simper?

SIR BENJAMIN

Why, she has very pretty teeth.

LADY TEAZLE

Yes; and on that account, when she is neither speaking nor laughing (which very seldom happens), she never absolutely shuts her mouth, but leaves it always on ajar, as it were—thus.   [*Shows her teeth.*

MRS. CANDOUR

How can you be so ill-natured?

LADY TEAZLE

Nay, I allow even that's better than the pains Mrs. Prim takes to conceal her losses in front. She draws her mouth till it positively resembles the aperture of a poor's-box, and all her words appear to slide out edgewise, as it were—thus: *How do you do, madam? Yes, madam.*

LADY SNEERWELL

Very well, Lady Teazle; I see you can be a little severe.

LADY TEAZLE

In defence of a friend it is but justice. But here comes Sir Peter to spoil our pleasantry.

Enter SIR PETER TEAZLE

SIR PETER

Ladies, your most obedient—[*Aside.*] Mercy on me, here is the whole set! a character dead at every word, I suppose.

MRS. CANDOUR

I am rejoiced you are come, Sir Peter. They have been so censorious—and Lady Teazle as bad as any one.

SIR PETER

That must be very distressing to you, Mrs. Candour, I dare swear.

MRS. CANDOUR

Oh, they will allow good qualities to nobody; not even good nature to our friend Mrs. Pursy.

LADY TEAZLE

What, the fat dowager who was at Mrs. Quadrille's last night?

MRS. CANDOUR

Nay, her bulk is her misfortune; and, when she takes so much pains to get rid of it, you ought not to reflect on her.

LADY SNEERWELL

That's very true, indeed.

LADY TEAZLE

Yes, I know she almost lives on acids and small whey; laces herself by pulleys; and often, in the hottest noon in summer, you may see her on a little squat pony, with her hair plaited up behind like a drummer's and puffing round the Ring on a full trot.

MRS. CANDOUR

I thank you, Lady Teazle, for defending her.

SIR PETER

Yes, a good defence, truly.

MRS. CANDOUR

Truly, Lady Teazle is as censorious as Miss Sallow.

CRABTREE

Yes, and she is a curious being to pretend to be censorious—an awkward gawky, without any one good point under heaven.

MRS. CANDOUR

Positively, you shall not be so very severe. Miss Sallow is a near relation of mine by marriage, and, as for her person, great allowance is to be made; for, let me tell you, a woman labours under many disadvantages who tries to pass for a girl of six-and-thirty.

LADY SNEERWELL

Though, surely, she is handsome still—and for the weakness in her eyes, considering how much she reads by candle-light, it is not to be wondered at.

MRS. CANDOUR

True; and then as to her manner, upon my word I think it is particularly graceful, considering she never had the least education; for you know her mother was a Welsh milliner, and her father a sugar-baker at Bristol.

SIR BENJAMIN

Ah! you are both of you too good-natured!

SIR PETER

Yes, damned good-natured! This their own relation! mercy on me!   [*Aside.*

MRS. CANDOUR

For my part, I own I cannot bear to hear a friend ill-spoken of.

SIR PETER

No, to be sure!

SIR BENJAMIN

Oh! you are of a moral turn. Mrs. Candour and I can sit for an hour and hear Lady Stucco talk sentiment.

LADY TEAZLE

Nay, I vow Lady Stucco is very well with the dessert after dinner; for she's just like the French fruit one cracks for mottoes—made up of paint and proverb.

MRS. CANDOUR

Well, I will never join in ridiculing a friend; and so I constantly tell my cousin Ogle, and you all know what pretensions she has to be critical on beauty.

CRABTREE

Oh, to be sure! she has herself the oddest countenance that ever was seen; 'tis a collection of features from all the different countries of the globe.

SIR BENJAMIN

So she has, indeed—an Irish front——

CRABTREE

Caledonian locks——

SIR BENJAMIN

Dutch nose——

CRABTREE
Austrian lips——

SIR BENJAMIN
Complexion of a Spaniard——

CRABTREE
And teeth *à la Chinoise*——

SIR BENJAMIN
In short, her face resembles a *table d'hôte* at Spa—
where no two guests are of a nation——

CRABTREE
Or a congress at the close of a general war—wherein
all the members, even to her eyes, appear to have a
different interest, and her nose and chin are the only
parties likely to join issue.

MRS. CANDOUR
Ha! ha! ha!

SIR PETER
Mercy on my life!—a person they dine with twice a
week!   [*Aside.*

LADY SNEERWELL
Go—go—you are a couple of provoking Toads.

MRS. CANDOUR
Nay, but I vow you shall not carry the laugh off so—
for give me leave to say, that Mrs. Ogle——

SIR PETER
Madam, madam, I beg your pardon—there's no stopping these good gentlemen's tongues. But when I tell
you, Mrs. Candour, that the lady they are abusing is
a particular friend of mine, I hope you'll not take her
part.

LADY SNEERWELL

Ha! ha! ha! well said, Sir Peter! but you are a cruel creature—too phlegmatic yourself for a jest, and too peevish to allow wit in others.

SIR PETER

Ah, madam, true wit is more nearly allied to good nature than your ladyship is aware of.

LADY TEAZLE

True, Sir Peter: I believe they are so near akin that they can never be united.

SIR BENJAMIN

Or rather, madam, suppose them man and wife, because one seldom sees them together.

LADY TEAZLE

But Sir Peter is such an enemy to scandal, I believe he would have it put down by parliament.

SIR PETER

'Fore heaven, madam, if they were to consider the sporting with reputation of as much importance as poaching on manors, and pass an act for the preservation of fame, I believe many would thank them for the bill.

LADY SNEERWELL

O Lud! Sir Peter; would you deprive us of our privileges?

SIR PETER

Ay, madam; and then no person should be permitted to kill characters and run down reputations, but qualified old maids and disappointed widows.

LADY SNEERWELL
Go, you monster!

MRS. CANDOUR
But, surely, you would not be quite so severe on those who only report what they hear?

SIR PETER
Yes, madam, I would have law merchant for them too; and in all cases of slander currency, whenever the drawer of the lie was not to be found, the injured parties should have a right to come on any of the indorsers.

CRABTREE
Well, for my part, I believe there never was a scandalous tale without some foundation.

LADY SNEERWELL
Come, ladies, shall we sit down to cards in the next room?

Enter SERVANT, *who whispers* SIR PETER

SIR PETER
I'll be with them directly.—[*Exit* SERVANT.] I'll get away unperceived.   [*Aside*.

LADY SNEERWELL
Sir Peter, you are not going to leave us?

SIR PETER
Your ladyship must excuse me; I'm called away by particular business. But I leave my character behind me.   [*Exit*.

MARIA

SIR BENJAMIN

Well—certainly, Lady Teazle, that lord of yours is a strange being: I could tell you some stories of him would make you laugh heartily if he were not your husband.

LADY TEAZLE

Oh, pray don't mind that; come, do let's hear them.
    [*Exeunt all but* JOSEPH SURFACE *and* MARIA.

JOSEPH SURFACE

Maria, I see you have no satisfaction in this society.

MARIA

How is it possible I should? If to raise malicious smiles at the infirmities or misfortunes of those who have never injured us be the province of wit or humour, Heaven grant me a double portion of dulness!

JOSEPH SURFACE

Yet they appear more ill-natured than they are; they have no malice at heart.

MARIA

Then is their conduct still more contemptible; for, in my opinion, nothing could excuse the intemperance of their tongues but a natural and uncontrollable bitterness of mind.

JOSEPH SURFACE

Undoubtedly, madam; and it has always been a sentiment of mine, that to propagate a malicious truth wantonly is more despicable than to falsify from revenge. But can you, Maria, feel thus for others, and be unkind to me alone? Is hope to be denied the tenderest passion?

MARIA

Why will you distress me by renewing this subject?

JOSEPH SURFACE

Ah, Maria! you would not treat me thus, and oppose your guardian, Sir Peter's will, but that I see that profligate Charles is still a favoured rival.

MARIA

Ungenerously urged! But, whatever my sentiments are for that unfortunate young man, be assured I shall not feel more bound to give him up, because his distresses have lost him the regard even of a brother.

JOSEPH SURFACE

Nay, but, Maria, do not leave me with a frown: by all that's honest, I swear—— 　　　　　　　　　　　[*Kneels.*

Re-enter LADY TEAZLE *behind*

[*Aside.*] Gad's life, here's Lady Teazle.—[*Aloud to* MARIA.] You must not—no, you shall not—for, though I have the greatest regard for Lady Teazle——

MARIA

Lady Teazle!

JOSEPH SURFACE

Yet were Sir Peter to suspect——

LADY TEAZLE

[*Coming forward.*] What is this, pray? Do you take her for me?—Child, you are wanted in the next room. —[*Exit* MARIA.] What is all this, pray?

JOSEPH SURFACE

Oh, the most unlucky circumstance in nature! Maria has somehow suspected the tender concern I have for your happiness, and threatened to acquaint Sir Peter with her suspicions, and I was just endeavouring to reason with her when you came in.

LADY TEAZLE

Indeed! but you seemed to adopt a very tender mode of reasoning—do you usually argue on your knees?

JOSEPH SURFACE

Oh, she's a child, and I thought a little bombast—— but, Lady Teazle, when are you to give me your judgment on my library, as you promised?

LADY TEAZLE

No, no; I begin to think it would be imprudent, and you know I admit you as a lover no farther than fashion requires.

JOSEPH SURFACE

True—a mere Platonic cicisbeo, what every wife is entitled to.

LADY TEAZLE

Certainly, one must not be out of the fashion. However, I have so many of my country prejudices left, that, though Sir Peter's ill humour may vex me ever so, it never shall provoke me to——

JOSEPH SURFACE

The only revenge in your power. Well, I applaud your moderation.

LADY TEAZLE

Go—you are an insinuating wretch! But we shall be missed—let us join the company.

JOSEPH SURFACE

But we had best not return together.

LADY TEAZLE

Well, don't stay; for Maria shan't come to hear any more of your reasoning, I promise you.   [*Exit.*

JOSEPH SURFACE

A curious dilemma, truly, my politics have run me into! I wanted, at first, only to ingratiate myself with Lady Teazle, that she might not be my enemy with Maria; and I have, I don't know how, become her serious lover. Sincerely I begin to wish I had never made such a point of gaining so very good a character, for it has led me into so many cursed rogueries that I doubt I shall be exposed at last.   [*Exit.*

SCENE THREE

A Room in SIR PETER TEAZLE'S *House*

Enter SIR OLIVER SURFACE *and* ROWLEY

SIR OLIVER

Ha! ha! ha! so my old friend is married, hey?—a young wife out of the country. Ha! ha! ha! that he should have stood bluff to old bachelor so long, and sink into a husband at last!

ROWLEY

But you must not rally him on the subject, Sir Oliver; 'tis a tender point, I assure you, though he has been married only seven months.

SIR OLIVER

Then he has been just half a year on the stool of repentance!—Poor Peter! But you say he has entirely given up Charles—never sees him, hey?

ROWLEY

His prejudice against him is astonishing, and I am sure greatly increased by a jealousy of him with Lady Teazle, which he has industriously been led into by a scandalous society in the neighbourhood, who have contributed not a little to Charles's ill name. Whereas the truth is, I believe, if the lady is partial to either of them, his brother is the favourite.

SIR OLIVER

Ay, I know there are a set of malicious, prating, prudent gossips, both male and female, who murder characters to kill time, and will rob a young fellow of his good name before he has years to know the value of it. But I am not to be prejudiced against my nephew by such, I promise you! No, no: if Charles has done nothing false or mean, I shall compound for his extravagance.

ROWLEY

Then, my life on't, you will reclaim him. Ah, sir, it gives me new life to find that your heart is not turned against him, and that the son of my good old master has one friend, however, left.

SIR OLIVER

What! shall I forget, Master Rowley, when I was at his years myself? Egad, my brother and I were neither of us very prudent youths; and yet, I believe, you have not seen many better men than your old master was?

ROWLEY

Sir, 'tis this reflection gives me assurance that Charles may yet be a credit to his family. But here comes Sir Peter.

SIR OLIVER

Egad, so he does! Mercy on me, he's greatly altered, and seems to have a settled married look! One may read husband in his face at this distance!

Enter SIR PETER TEAZLE

SIR PETER

Ha! Sir Oliver—my old friend! Welcome to England a thousand times!

SIR OLIVER

Thank you, thank you, Sir Peter! and i'faith I am glad to find you well, believe me!

SIR PETER

Oh! 'tis a long time since we met—fifteen years, I doubt, Sir Oliver, and many a cross accident in the time.

SIR OLIVER

Ay, I have had my share. But, what! I find you are married, hey, my old boy? Well, well, it can't be helped; and so—I wish you joy with all my heart!

SIR PETER

Thank you, thank you, Sir Oliver.—Yes, I have entered into—the happy state; but we'll not talk of that now.

SIR OLIVER

True, true, Sir Peter; old friends should not begin on grievances at first meeting. No, no, no.

ROWLEY

[*Aside to* SIR OLIVER.] Take care, pray, sir.

SIR OLIVER

Well, so one of my nephews is a wild rogue, hey?

SIR PETER

Wild! Ah! my old friend, I grieve for your disappointment there; he's a lost young man, indeed. However, his brother will make you amends; Joseph is, indeed, what a youth should be—everybody in the world speaks well of him.

SIR OLIVER

I am sorry to hear it; he has too good a character to be an honest fellow. Everybody speaks well of him! Psha! then he has bowed as low to knaves and fools as to the honest dignity of genius and virtue.

SIR PETER

What, Sir Oliver! do you blame him for not making enemies?

SIR OLIVER

Yes, if he has merit enough to deserve them.

SIR PETER

Well, well—you'll be convinced when you know him. 'Tis edification to hear him converse; he professes the noblest sentiments.

223

SIR OLIVER

Oh, plague of his sentiments! If he salutes me with a scrap of morality in his mouth, I shall be sick directly. But, however, don't mistake me, Sir Peter; I don't mean to defend Charles's errors: but, before I form my judgment of either of them, I intend to make a trial of their hearts; and my friend Rowley and I have planned something for the purpose.

ROWLEY

And Sir Peter shall own for once he has been mistaken.

SIR PETER

Oh, my life on Joseph's honour!

SIR OLIVER

Well—come, give us a bottle of good wine, and we'll drink the lads' health, and tell you our scheme.

SIR PETER

Allons, then!

SIR OLIVER

And don't, Sir Peter, be so severe against your old friend's son. Odds my life! I am not sorry that he has run out of the course a little: for my part, I hate to see prudence clinging to the green suckers of youth; 'tis like ivy round a sapling, and spoils the growth of the tree. *[Exeunt.*

ACT THREE

SCENE ONE

A Room in SIR PETER TEAZLE'S *House*

Enter SIR PETER TEAZLE, SIR OLIVER SURFACE,
and ROWLEY

SIR PETER

Well, then, we will see this fellow first, and have our wine afterwards. But how is this, Master Rowley? I don't see the jet of your scheme.

ROWLEY

Why, sir, this Mr. Stanley, whom I was speaking of, is nearly related to them by their mother. He was once a merchant in Dublin, but has been ruined by a series of undeserved misfortunes. He has applied, by letter, since his confinement, both to Mr. Surface and Charles: from the former he has received nothing but evasive promises of future service, while Charles has done all that his extravagance has left him power to do; and he is, at this time, endeavouring to raise a sum of money, part of which, in the midst of his own distresses, I know he intends for the service of poor Stanley.

SIR OLIVER

Ah! he is my brother's son.

SIR PETER

Well, but how is Sir Oliver personally to——

ROWLEY

Why, sir, I will inform Charles and his brother that Stanley has obtained permission to apply personally to his friends; and, as they have neither of them ever seen him, let Sir Oliver assume his character, and he will have a fair opportunity of judging, at least, of the benevolence of their dispositions: and believe me, sir, you will find in the youngest brother one who, in the midst of folly and dissipation, has still, as our immortal bard expresses it,—

'a heart to pity, and a hand
Open as day, for melting charity.'

SIR PETER

Psha! What signifies his having an open hand or purse either, when he has nothing left to give? Well, well, make the trial, if you please. But where is the fellow whom you brought for Sir Oliver to examine, relative to Charles's affairs?

ROWLEY

Below, waiting his commands, and no one can give him better intelligence.—This, Sir Oliver, is a friendly Jew, who, to do him justice, has done everything in his power to bring your nephew to a proper sense of his extravagance.

SIR PETER

Pray let us have him in.

ROWLEY

Desire Mr. Moses to walk upstairs.

[*Calls to* SERVANT.

226

SIR PETER

But, pray, why should you suppose he will speak the truth?

ROWLEY

Oh, I have convinced him that he has no chance of recovering certain sums advanced to Charles but through the bounty of Sir Oliver, who he knows is arrived; so that you may depend on his fidelity to his own interests. I have also another evidence in my power, one Snake, whom I have detected in a matter little short of forgery, and shall shortly produce to remove some of your prejudices, Sir Peter, relative to Charles and Lady Teazle.

SIR PETER

I have heard too much on that subject.

ROWLEY

Here comes the honest Israelite.

Enter MOSES

—This is Sir Oliver.

SIR OLIVER

Sir, I understand you have lately had great dealings with my nephew Charles.

MOSES

Yes, Sir Oliver, I have done all I could for him; but he was ruined before he came to me for assistance.

SIR OLIVER

That was unlucky, truly; for you have had no opportunity of showing your talents.

227

MOSES

None at all; I hadn't the pleasure of knowing his distresses till he was some thousands worse than nothing.

SIR OLIVER

Unfortunate, indeed! But I suppose you have done all in your power for him, honest Moses?

MOSES

Yes, he knows that. This very evening I was to have brought him a gentleman from the city, who does not know him, and will, I believe, advance him some money.

SIR PETER

What, one Charles has never had money from before?

MOSES

Yes, Mr. Premium, of Crutched Friars, formerly a broker.

SIR PETER

Egad, Sir Oliver, a thought strikes me!—Charles, you say, does not know Mr. Premium?

MOSES

Not at all.

SIR PETER

Now then, Sir Oliver, you may have a better opportunity of satisfying yourself than by an old romancing tale of a poor relation: go with my friend Moses, and represent Premium, and then, I'll answer for it, you'll see your nephew in all his glory.

SIR OLIVER

Egad, I like this idea better than the other, and I may visit Joseph afterwards as old Stanley.

SIR PETER

True—so you may.

ROWLEY

Well, this is taking Charles rather at a disadvantage, to be sure. However, Moses, you understand Sir Peter, and will be faithful?

MOSES

You may depend upon me.—[*Looks at his watch.*] This is near the time I was to have gone.

SIR OLIVER

I'll accompany you as soon as you please, Moses—— But hold! I have forgot one thing—how the plague shall I be able to pass for a Jew?

MOSES

There's no need—the principal is Christian.

SIR OLIVER

Is he? I'm very sorry to hear it. But, then again, an't I rather too smartly dressed to look like a money-lender?

SIR PETER

Not at all; 'twould not be out of character, if you went in your carriage—would it, Moses?

MOSES

Not in the least.

SIR OLIVER

Well, but how must I talk? there's certainly some cant of usury and mode of treating that I ought to know.

SIR PETER

Oh, there's not much to learn. The great point, as I take it, is to be exorbitant enough in your demands. Hey, Moses?

MOSES

Yes, that's a very great point.

SIR OLIVER

I'll answer for't I'll not be wanting in that. I'll ask him eight or ten per cent. on the loan, at least.

MOSES

If you ask him no more than that, you'll be discovered immediately.

SIR OLIVER

Hey! what, the plague! how much then?

MOSES

That depends upon the circumstances. If he appears not very anxious for the supply, you should require only forty or fifty per cent.; but if you find him in great distress, and want the moneys very bad, you may ask double.

SIR PETER

A good honest trade you're learning, Sir Oliver!

SIR OLIVER

Truly I think so—and not unprofitable.

MOSES

Then, you know, you haven't the moneys yourself, but are forced to borrow them for him of a friend.

SIR OLIVER

Oh! I borrow it of a friend, do I?

MOSES

And your friend is an unconscionable dog: but you can't help that.

SIR OLIVER

My friend an unconscionable dog, is he?

MOSES

Yes, and he himself has not the moneys by him, but is forced to sell stock at a great loss.

SIR OLIVER

He is forced to sell stock at a great loss, is he? Well, that's very kind of him.

SIR PETER

I'faith, Sir Oliver—Mr. Premium, I mean—you'll soon be master of the trade. But, Moses! would not you have him run out a little against the annuity bill? That would be in character, I should think.

MOSES

Very much.

ROWLEY

And lament that a young man now must be at years of discretion before he is suffered to ruin himself?

MOSES

Ay, great pity!

SIR PETER

And abuse the public for allowing merit to an act whose only object is to snatch misfortune and imprudence from the rapacious grip of usury, and give the minor a chance of inheriting his estate without being undone by coming into possession.

SIR OLIVER

So, so—Moses shall give me further instructions as we go together.

SIR PETER

You will not have much time, for your nephew lives hard by.

SIR OLIVER

Oh, never fear! my tutor appears so able, that though Charles lived in the next street, it must be my own fault if I am not a complete rogue before I turn the corner.   [*Exit with* MOSES.

SIR PETER

So, now, I think Sir Oliver will be convinced: you are partial, Rowley, and would have prepared Charles for the other plot.

ROWLEY

No, upon my word, Sir Peter.

SIR PETER

Well, go bring me this Snake, and I'll hear what he has to say presently. I see Maria, and want to speak with her.—[*Exit* ROWLEY.] I should be glad to be convinced my suspicions of Lady Teazle and Charles were unjust. I have never yet opened my mind on this subject to my friend Joseph—I am determined I will do it—he will give me his opinion sincerely.

ROWLEY

Enter MARIA

So, child, has Mr. Surface returned with you?

MARIA

No, sir; he was engaged.

SIR PETER

Well, Maria, do you not reflect, the more you converse with that amiable young man, what return his
partiality for you deserves?

MARIA

Indeed, Sir Peter, your frequent importunity on this
subject distresses me extremely—you compel me to
declare, that I know no man who has ever paid me a
particular attention whom I would not prefer to
Mr. Surface.

SIR PETER

So—here's perverseness! No, no, Maria, 'tis Charles
only whom you would prefer. 'Tis evident his vices
and follies have won your heart.

MARIA

This is unkind, sir. You know I have obeyed you
in neither seeing nor corresponding with him: I have
heard enough to convince me that he is unworthy my
regard. Yet I cannot think it culpable, if, while my
understanding severely condemns his vices, my heart
suggests pity for his distresses.

SIR PETER

Well, well, pity him as much as you please; but give
your heart and hand to a worthier object.

MARIA

Never to his brother!

SIR PETER

Go, perverse and obstinate! But take care, madam; you have never yet known what the authority of a guardian is: don't compel me to inform you of it.

MARIA

I can only say, you shall not have just reason. 'Tis true, by my father's will, I am for a short period bound to regard you as his substitute; but must cease to think you so, when you would compel me to be miserable. [*Exit*.

SIR PETER

Was ever man so crossed as I am, everything conspiring to fret me! I had not been involved in matrimony a fortnight, before her father, a hale and hearty man, died, on purpose, I believe, for the pleasure of plaguing me with the care of his daughter.—[LADY TEAZLE *sings without*.] But here comes my helpmate! She appears in great good humour. How happy I should be if I could tease her into loving me, though but a little!

Enter LADY TEAZLE

LADY TEAZLE

Lud! Sir Peter, I hope you haven't been quarrelling with Maria? It is not using me well to be ill humoured when I am not by.

SIR PETER

Ah, Lady Teazle, you might have the power to make me good humoured at all times.

LADY TEAZLE

I am sure I wish I had; for I want you to be in a charming sweet temper at this moment. Do be good

234

humoured now, and let me have two hundred pounds, will you?

SIR PETER

Two hundred pounds; what, an't I to be in a good humour without paying for it! But speak to me thus, and i'faith there's nothing I could refuse you. You shall have it; but seal me a bond for the repayment.

LADY TEAZLE

Oh, no—there—my note of hand will do as well.

[Offering her hand.

SIR PETER

And you shall no longer reproach me with not giving you an independent settlement. I mean shortly to surprise you; but shall we always live thus, hey?

LADY TEAZLE

If you please. I'm sure I don't care how soon we leave off quarrelling, provided you'll own you were tired first.

SIR PETER

Well—then let our future contest be, who shall be most obliging.

LADY TEAZLE

I assure you, Sir Peter, good nature becomes you. You look now as you did before we were married, when you used to walk with me under the elms, and tell me stories of what a gallant you were in your youth, and chuck me under the chin, you would; and ask me if I thought I could love an old fellow, who would deny me nothing—didn't you?

SIR PETER

Yes, yes, and you were as kind and attentive——

LADY TEAZLE

Ay, so I was, and would always take your part, when my acquaintance used to abuse you, and turn you into ridicule.

SIR PETER

Indeed!

LADY TEAZLE

Ay, and when my cousin Sophy has called you a stiff, peevish old bachelor, and laughed at me for thinking of marrying one who might be my father, I have always defended you, and said, I didn't think you so ugly by any means, and that you'd make a very good sort of a husband.

SIR PETER

And you prophesied right; and we shall now be the happiest couple——

LADY TEAZLE

And never differ again?

SIR PETER

No, never—though at the same time, indeed, my dear Lady Teazle, you must watch your temper very seriously; for in all our little quarrels, my dear, if you recollect, my love, you always began first.

LADY TEAZLE

I beg your pardon, my dear Sir Peter: indeed, you always gave the provocation.

SIR PETER

Now, see, my angel! take care—contradicting isn't the way to keep friends.

LADY TEAZLE

Then, don't you begin it, my love!

SIR PETER

There, now! you—you are going on. You don't perceive, my life, that you are just doing the very thing
which you know always makes me angry.

LADY TEAZLE

Nay, you know if you will be angry without any
reason, my dear——

SIR PETER

There! now you want to quarrel again.

LADY TEAZLE

No, I'm sure I don't: but, if you will be so peevish——

SIR PETER

There now! who begins first?

LADY TEAZLE

Why, you, to be sure. I said nothing—but there's no
bearing your temper.

SIR PETER

No, no, madam: the fault's in your own temper.

LADY TEAZLE

Ay, you are just what my cousin Sophy said you
would be.

SIR PETER

Your cousin Sophy is a forward, impertinent gipsy.

LADY TEAZLE

You are a great bear, I am sure, to abuse my
relations.

SIR PETER

Now may all the plagues of marriage be doubled on me, if ever I try to be friends with you any more!

LADY TEAZLE

So much the better.

SIR PETER

No, no, madam: 'tis evident you never cared a pin for me, and I was a madman to marry you—a pert, rural coquette, that had refused half the honest 'squires in the neighbourhood!

LADY TEAZLE

And I am sure I was a fool to marry you—an old dangling bachelor, who was single at fifty, only because he never could meet with any one who would have him.

SIR PETER

Ay, ay, madam; but you were pleased enough to listen to me: you never had such an offer before.

LADY TEAZLE

No! didn't I refuse Sir Tivy Terrier, who everybody said would have been a better match? for his estate is just as good as yours, and he has broke his neck since we have been married.

SIR PETER

I have done with you, madam! You are an unfeeling, ungrateful—but there's an end of everything. I believe you capable of everything that is bad. Yes, madam, I now believe the reports relative to you and Charles, madam. Yes, madam, you and Charles are, not without grounds——

LADY TEAZLE

Take care, Sir Peter! you had better not insinuate any such thing! I'll not be suspected without cause, I promise you.

SIR PETER

Very well, madam! very well! a separate maintenance as soon as you please. Yes, madam, or a divorce! I'll make an example of myself for the benefit of all old bachelors. Let us separate, madam.

LADY TEAZLE

Agreed! agreed! And now, my dear Sir Peter, we are of a mind once more, we may be the happiest couple, and never differ again, you know: ha! ha! ha! Well, you are going to be in a passion, I see, and I shall only interrupt you—so, bye! bye!   [*Exit.*

SIR PETER

Plagues and tortures! can't I make her angry either! Oh, I am the most miserable fellow! But I'll not bear her presuming to keep her temper: no! she may break my heart, but she shan't keep her temper.   [*Exit.*

SCENE TWO

A Room in CHARLES SURFACE'S *House*

Enter TRIP, MOSES, *and* SIR OLIVER SURFACE

TRIP

Here, Master Moses! if you'll stay a moment, I'll try whether—what's the gentleman's name?

SIR OLIVER

Mr. Moses, what is my name?   [*Aside to* MOSES.

MOSES

Mr. Premium.

TRIP

Premium—very well.   [*Exit, taking snuff.*

SIR OLIVER

To judge by the servants, one wouldn't believe the master was ruined. But what!—sure, this was my brother's house?

MOSES

Yes, sir; Mr. Charles bought it of Mr. Joseph, with the furniture, pictures, etc., just as the old gentleman left it. Sir Peter thought it a piece of extravagance in him.

SIR OLIVER

In my mind, the other's economy in selling it to him was more reprehensible by half.

Re-enter TRIP

TRIP

My master says you must wait, gentlemen: he has company, and can't speak with you yet.

SIR OLIVER

If he knew who it was wanted to see him, perhaps he would not send such a message?

TRIP

Yes, yes, sir; he knows you are here—I did not forget little Premium: no, no, no.

SIR OLIVER

Very well; and I pray, sir, what may be your name?

TRIP

Trip, sir; my name is Trip, at your service.

Sir Oliver Surface

SIR OLIVER

Well, then, Mr. Trip, you have a pleasant sort of place here, I guess?

TRIP

Why, yes—here are three or four of us pass our time agreeably enough; but then our wages are sometimes a little in arrear—and not very great either—but fifty pounds a year, and find our own bags and bouquets.

SIR OLIVER

Bags and bouquets! halters and bastinadoes!

[*Aside.*

TRIP

And *à propos*, Moses, have you been able to get me that little bill discounted?

SIR OLIVER

Wants to raise money, too!—mercy on me! Has his distresses too, I warrant, like a lord, and affects creditors and duns.   [*Aside.*

MOSES

'Twas not to be done, indeed, Mr. Trip.

TRIP

Good lack, you surprise me! My friend Brush has indorsed it, and I thought when he put his name at the back of a bill 'twas the same as cash.

MOSES

No, 'twouldn't do.

TRIP

A small sum—but twenty pounds. Hark'ee, Moses, do you think you couldn't get it me by way of annuity?

SIR OLIVER

An annuity! ha! ha! a footman raise money by way of annuity! Well done, luxury, egad!   [*Aside.*

MOSES

Well, but you must insure your place.

TRIP

Oh, with all my heart! I'll insure my place, and my life too, if you please.

SIR OLIVER

It's more than I would your neck.   [*Aside.*

MOSES

But is there nothing you could deposit?

TRIP

Why, nothing capital of my master's wardrobe has dropped lately; but I could give you a mortgage on some of his winter clothes, with equity of redemption before November—or you shall have the reversion of the French velvet, or a post-obit on the blue and silver;—these, I should think, Moses, with a few pair of point ruffles, as a collateral security—hey, my little fellow?

MOSES

Well, well.   [*Bell rings.*

TRIP

Egad, I heard the bell! I believe, gentlemen, I can now introduce you. Don't forget the annuity, little Moses! This way, gentlemen, I'll insure my place, you know.

SIR OLIVER

[*Aside.*] If the man be a shadow of the master, this is the temple of dissipation indeed!   [*Exeunt.*

SCENE THREE
Another Room in the same

CHARLES SURFACE, SIR HARRY BUMPER,
CARELESS, *and* GENTLEMEN, *discovered drinking*

CHARLES SURFACE

'Fore heaven, 'tis true!—there's the great degeneracy of the age. Many of our acquaintance have taste, spirit, and politeness; but plague on't they won't drink.

CARELESS

It is so, indeed, Charles! they give in to all the substantial luxuries of the table, and abstain from nothing but wine and wit. Oh, certainly society suffers by it intolerably! for now, instead of the social spirit of raillery that used to mantle over a glass of bright Burgundy, their conversation is become just like the Spa-water they drink, which has all the pertness and flatulency of champagne, without its spirit or flavour.

FIRST GENTLEMAN

But what are they to do who love play better than wine?

CARELESS

True! there's Sir Harry diets himself for gaming, and is now under a hazard regimen.

CHARLES SURFACE

Then he'll have the worst of it. What! you wouldn't train a horse for the course by keeping him from corn? For my part, egad, I'm never so successful as when I am a little merry: let me throw on a bottle of champagne, and I never lose—at least I never feel my losses, which is exactly the same thing.

SECOND GENTLEMAN

Ay, that I believe.

CHARLES SURFACE

And, then, what man can pretend to be a believer in love, who is an abjurer of wine? 'Tis the test by which the lover knows his own heart. Fill a dozen bumpers to a dozen beauties, and she that floats at the top is the maid that has bewitched you.

CARELESS

Now then, Charles, be honest, and give us your real favourite.

CHARLES SURFACE

Why, I have withheld her only in compassion to you. If I toast her, you must give a round of her peers, which is impossible—on earth.

CARELESS

Oh, then we'll find some canonised vestals or heathen goddesses that will do, I warrant!

CHARLES SURFACE

Here then, bumpers, you rogues! bumpers! Maria! Maria—

SIR HARRY

Maria who?

CHARLES SURFACE

Oh, damn the surname!—'tis too formal to be registered in Love's calendar—but now, Sir Harry, beware, we must have beauty superlative.

CARELESS

Nay, never study, Sir Harry: we'll stand to the toast, though your mistress should want an eye, and you know you have a song will excuse you.

SIR HARRY

Egad, so I have! and I'll give him the song instead of
the lady.   [*Sings.*

     Here's to the maiden of bashful fifteen;
        Here's to the widow of fifty;
     Here's to the flaunting extravagant quean,
        And here's to the housewife that's thrifty.

Chorus.   Let the toast pass,—
           Drink to the lass,
I'll warrant she'll prove an excuse for a glass.

     Here's to the charmer whose dimples we prize;
        Now to the maid who has none, sir;
     Here's to the girl with a pair of blue eyes,
        And here's to the nymph with but one, sir.

Chorus.   Let the toast pass,—
           Drink to the lass,
I'll warrant she'll prove an excuse for a glass.

     Here's to the maid with a bosom of snow:
        Now to her that's as brown as a berry:
     Here's to the wife with a face full of woe,
        And now to the damsel that's merry.

Chorus.   Let the toast pass,—
           Drink to the lass,
I'll warrant she'll prove an excuse for a glass.

For let 'em be clumsy, or let 'em be slim,
    Young or ancient, I care not a feather;
So fill a pint bumper quite up to the brim,
So fill up your glasses, nay, fill to the brim,
    And let us e'en toast them together.

Chorus.   Let the toast pass,—
        Drink to the lass,
I'll warrant she'll prove an excuse for a glass.

ALL
Bravo! Bravo!

Enter TRIP, *and whispers* CHARLES SURFACE

CHARLES SURFACE
Gentlemen, you must excuse me a little.—Careless, take the chair, will you?

CARELESS
Nay, pr'ythee, Charles, what now? This is one of your peerless beauties, I suppose, dropped in by chance?

CHARLES SURFACE
No, faith! To tell you the truth, 'tis a Jew and a broker, who are come by appointment.

CARELESS
Oh, damn it! let's have the Jew in.

FIRST GENTLEMAN
Ay, and the broker too, by all means.

SECOND GENTLEMAN
Yes, yes, the Jew and the broker.

CHARLES SURFACE

Egad, with all my heart!—Trip, bid the gentlemen walk in.—[*Exit* TRIP.] Though there's one of them a stranger, I can tell you.

CARELESS

Charles, let us give them some generous Burgundy, and perhaps they'll grow conscientious.

CHARLES SURFACE

Oh, hang 'em, no! wine does but draw forth a man's natural qualities; and to make them drink would only be to whet their knavery.

Re-enter TRIP, *with* SIR OLIVER SURFACE *and* MOSES

CHARLES SURFACE

So, honest Moses; walk in, pray, Mr. Premium—that's the gentleman's name, isn't it, Moses?

MOSES

Yes, sir.

CHARLES SURFACE

Set chairs, Trip.—Sit down, Mr. Premium.—Glasses, Trip.—[TRIP *gives chairs and glasses, and exit.*] Sit down, Moses.—Come, Mr. Premium, I'll give you a sentiment; here's *Success to usury!*—Moses, fill the gentleman a bumper.

MOSES

Success to usury!   [*Drinks.*

CARELESS

Right, Moses—usury is prudence and industry, and deserves to succeed.

247

SIR OLIVER

Then here's—All the success it deserves! [*Drinks.*

CARELESS

No, no, that won't do! Mr. Premium, you have demurred at the toast, and must drink it in a pint bumper.

FIRST GENTLEMAN

A pint bumper, at least.

MOSES

Oh, pray, sir, consider—Mr. Premium's a gentleman.

CARELESS

And therefore loves good wine.

SECOND GENTLEMAN

Give Moses a quart glass—this is mutiny, and a high contempt for the chair.

CARELESS

Here, now for't! I'll see justice done, to the last drop of my bottle.

SIR OLIVER

Nay, pray, gentlemen—I did not expect this usage.

CHARLES SURFACE

No, hang it, you shan't; Mr. Premium's a stranger.

SIR OLIVER

Odd! I wish I was well out of their company. [*Aside.*

CARELESS

Plague on 'em then! if they won't drink, we'll not sit down with them. Come, Harry, the dice are in the next room.—Charles, you'll join us when you have finished your business with the gentlemen?

CHARLES SURFACE

I will! I will!—[*Exeunt* SIR HARRY BUMPER *and* GENTLEMEN; CARELESS *following.*] Careless.

CARELESS

[*Returning.*] Well!

CHARLES SURFACE

Perhaps I may want you.

CARELESS

Oh, you know I am always ready: word, note, or bond, 'tis all the same to me.   [*Exit.*

MOSES

Sir, this is Mr. Premium, a gentleman of the strictest honour and secrecy; and always performs what he undertakes. Mr. Premium, this is——

CHARLES SURFACE

Psha! have done. Sir, my friend Moses is a very honest fellow, but a little slow at expression: he'll be an hour giving us our titles. Mr. Premium, the plain state of the matter is this: I am an extravagant young fellow who wants to borrow money; you I take to be a prudent old fellow, who has got money to lend. I am blockhead enough to give fifty per cent. sooner than not have it! and you, I presume, are rogue enough to take a hundred if you can get it. Now, sir, you see we are acquainted at once, and may proceed to business without further ceremony.

SIR OLIVER

Exceeding frank, upon my word. I see, sir, you are not a man of many compliments.

CHARLES SURFACE

Oh, no, sir! plain dealing in business I always think best.

SIR OLIVER

Sir, I like you the better for it. However, you are mistaken in one thing; I have no money to lend, but I believe I could procure some of a friend; but then he's an unconscionable dog. Isn't he, Moses? And must sell stock to accommodate you. Mustn't he, Moses?

MOSES

Yes, indeed! You know I always speak the truth, and scorn to tell a lie!

CHARLES SURFACE

Right. People that speak truth generally do. But these are trifles, Mr. Premium. What! I know money isn't to be bought without paying for't!

SIR OLIVER

Well, but what security could you give? You have no land, I suppose?

CHARLES SURFACE

Not a mole-hill, nor a twig, but what's in the bough-pots out of the window!

SIR OLIVER

Nor any stock, I presume?

CHARLES SURFACE

Nothing but live stock—and that's only a few pointers and ponies. But pray, Mr. Premium, are you acquainted at all with any of my connections?

SIR OLIVER

Why, to say the truth, I am.

CHARLES SURFACE

Then you must know that I have a devilish rich uncle in the East Indies, Sir Oliver Surface, from whom I have the greatest expectations?

SIR OLIVER

That you have a wealthy uncle, I have heard; but how your expectations will turn out is more, I believe, than you can tell.

CHARLES SURFACE

Oh, no!—there can be no doubt. They tell me I'm a prodigious favourite, and that he talks of leaving me everything.

SIR OLIVER

Indeed! this is the first I've heard of it.

CHARLES SURFACE

Yes, yes, 'tis just so. Moses knows 'tis true; don't you, Moses?

MOSES

Oh, yes! I'll swear to't.

SIR OLIVER

Egad, they'll persuade me presently I'm at Bengal.

[*Aside.*

CHARLES SURFACE

Now I propose, Mr. Premium, if it's agreeable to you, a post-obit on Sir Oliver's life: though at the same time the old fellow has been so liberal to me, that I give you my word, I should be very sorry to hear that anything had happened to him.

SIR OLIVER

Not more than I should, I assure you. But the bond you mention happens to be just the worst security you could offer me—for I might live to a hundred and never see the principal.

CHARLES SURFACE

Oh, yes, you would! the moment Sir Oliver dies, you know, you would come on me for the money.

SIR OLIVER

Then I believe I should be the most unwelcome dun you ever had in your life.

CHARLES SURFACE

What! I suppose you're afraid that Sir Oliver is too good a life?

SIR OLIVER

No, indeed I am not; though I have heard he is as hale and healthy as any man of his years in Christendom.

CHARLES SURFACE

There again, now, you are misinformed. No, no, the climate has hurt him considerably, poor uncle Oliver. Yes, yes, he breaks apace, I'm told—and is so much altered lately that his nearest relations would not know him.

SIR OLIVER

No! Ha! ha! ha! so much altered lately that his nearest relations would not know him! Ha! ha! ha! egad—ha! ha! ha!

CHARLES SURFACE

Ha! ha!—you're glad to hear that, little Premium?

SIR OLIVER
No, no, I'm not.

CHARLES SURFACE
Yes, yes, you are—ha! ha! ha!—you know that mends your chance.

SIR OLIVER
But I'm told Sir Oliver is coming over; nay, some say he has actually arrived.

CHARLES SURFACE
Psha! sure I must know better than you whether he's come or not. No, no, rely on't he's at this moment at Calcutta. Isn't he, Moses?

MOSES
Oh, yes, certainly.

SIR OLIVER
Very true, as you say, you must know better than I, though I have it from pretty good authority. Haven't I, Moses?

MOSES
Yes, most undoubted!

SIR OLIVER
But, sir, as I understand you want a few hundreds immediately, is there nothing you could dispose of?

CHARLES SURFACE
How do you mean?

SIR OLIVER
For instance, now, I have heard that your father left behind him a great quantity of massy old plate.

CHARLES SURFACE

O Lud! that's gone long ago. Moses can tell you how better than I can.

SIR OLIVER

[*Aside.*] Good lack! all the family race-cups and corporation-bowls!—[*Aloud.*] Then it was also supposed that his library was one of the most valuable and compact.

CHARLES SURFACE

Yes, yes, so it was—vastly too much so for a private gentleman. For my part, I was always of a communicative disposition, so I thought it a shame to keep so much knowledge to myself.

SIR OLIVER

[*Aside.*] Mercy upon me! learning that had run in the family like an heir-loom!—[*Aloud.*] Pray, what has become of the books?

CHARLES SURFACE

You must inquire of the auctioneer, Master Premium, for I don't believe even Moses can direct you.

MOSES

I know nothing of books.

SIR OLIVER

So, so, nothing of the family property left, I suppose?

CHARLES SURFACE

Not much, indeed; unless you have a mind to the family pictures. I have got a room full of ancestors above: and if you have a taste for old paintings, egad, you shall have 'em a bargain!

SIR OLIVER

Hey! what the devil! sure, you wouldn't sell your forefathers, would you?

CHARLES SURFACE

Every man of them, to the best bidder.

SIR OLIVER

What! your great-uncles and aunts?

CHARLES SURFACE

Ay, and my great-grandfathers and grandmothers too.

SIR OLIVER

[*Aside.*] Now I give him up!—[*Aloud.*] What the plague, have you no bowels for your own kindred? Odd's life! do you take me for Shylock in the play, that you would raise money of me on your own flesh and blood?

CHARLES SURFACE

Nay, my little broker, don't be angry: what need you care, if you have your money's worth?

SIR OLIVER

Well, I'll be the purchaser: I think I can dispose of the family canvas.—[*Aside.*] Oh, I'll never forgive him this! never!

Re-enter CARELESS

CARELESS

Come, Charles, what keeps you?

CHARLES SURFACE

I can't come yet. I'faith, we are going to have a sale above stairs, here's little Premium will buy all my ancestors!

255

CARELESS

Oh, burn your ancestors!

CHARLES SURFACE

No, he may do that afterwards, if he pleases. Stay, Careless, we want you: egad, you shall be auctioneer —so come along with us.

CARELESS

Oh, have with you, if that's the case. I can handle a hammer as well as a dice box! Going! going!

SIR OLIVER

Oh, the profligates!   [*Aside.*

CHARLES SURFACE

Come, Moses, you shall be appraiser, if we want one. Gad's life, little Premium, you don't seem to like the business?

SIR OLIVER

Oh, yes, I do, vastly! Ha! ha! ha! yes, yes, I think it a rare joke to sell one's family by auction—ha! ha!— [*Aside.*] Oh, the prodigal!

CHARLES SURFACE

To be sure! when a man wants money, where the plague should he get assistance, if he can't make free with his own relations?   [*Exeunt.*

SIR OLIVER

I'll never forgive him; never! never!

MOSES

ACT FOUR

SCENE ONE

A Picture Room in CHARLES SURFACE'S *House*

Enter CHARLES SURFACE, SIR OLIVER SURFACE,
MOSES, *and* CARELESS

CHARLES SURFACE

Walk in, gentlemen, pray walk in;—here they are, the family of the Surfaces, up to the Conquest.

SIR OLIVER

And, in my opinion, a goodly collection.

CHARLES SURFACE

Ay, ay, these are done in the true spirit of portrait-painting; no *volontière grace* or expression. Not like the works of your modern Raphaels, who give you the strongest resemblance, yet contrive to make your portrait independent of you; so that you may sink the original and not hurt the picture. No, no; the merit of these is the inveterate likeness—all stiff and awkward as the originals, and like nothing in human nature besides.

SIR OLIVER

Ah! we shall never see such figures of men again.

CHARLES SURFACE

I hope not. Well, you see, Master Premium, what a domestic character I am; here I sit of an evening surrounded by my family. But come, get to your pulpit, Mr. Auctioneer; here's an old gouty chair of my grandfather's will answer the purpose.

CARELESS

Ay, ay, this will do. But, Charles, I haven't a hammer; and what's an auctioneer without his hammer?

CHARLES SURFACE

Egad, that's true. What parchment have we here? Oh, our genealogy in full. [*Taking pedigree down.*] Here, Careless, you shall have no common bit of mahogany, here's the family tree for you, you rogue! This shall be your hammer, and now you may knock down my ancestors with their own pedigree.

SIR OLIVER

What an unnatural rogue!—an *ex post facto* parricide!
[*Aside.*

CARELESS

Yes, yes, here's a list of your generation indeed;—faith, Charles, this is the most convenient thing you could have found for the business, for 'twill not only serve as a hammer, but a catalogue into the bargain. Come, begin—A-going, a-going, a-going!

CHARLES SURFACE

Bravo, Careless! Well, here's my great uncle, Sir Richard Ravelin, a marvellous good general in his day, I assure you. He served in all the Duke of Marlborough's wars, and got that cut over his eye at the battle of Malplaquet. What say you, Mr. Premium? look at him—there's a hero! not cut out of his feathers, as your modern clipped captains are, but enveloped in wig and regimentals, as a general should be. What do you bid?

SIR OLIVER

[*Aside to* MOSES.] Bid him speak.

MOSES

Mr. Premium would have you speak.

CHARLES SURFACE

Why, then, he shall have him for ten pounds, and I'm sure that's not dear for a staff-officer.

SIR OLIVER

[*Aside.*] Heaven deliver me! his famous uncle Richard for ten pounds!—[*Aloud.*] Very well, sir, I take him at that.

CHARLES SURFACE

Careless, knock down my uncle Richard.—Here, now, is a maiden sister of his, my great-aunt Deborah, done by Kneller, in his best manner, and esteemed a very formidable likeness. There she is, you see, a shepherdess feeding her flock. You shall have her for five pounds ten—the sheep are worth the money.

SIR OLIVER

[*Aside.*] Ah! poor Deborah! a woman who set such a value on herself!—[*Aloud.*] Five pounds ten—she's mine.

CHARLES SURFACE

Knock down my aunt Deborah! Here, now, are two that were a sort of cousins of theirs.—You see, Moses, these pictures were done some time ago, when beaux wore wigs, and the ladies their own hair.

SIR OLIVER
Yes, truly, head-dresses appear to have been a little lower in those days.

CHARLES SURFACE
Well, take that couple for the same.

MOSES
'Tis a good bargain.

CHARLES SURFACE
Careless!—This, now, is a grandfather of my mother's, a learned judge, well known on the western circuit.—What do you rate him at, Moses?

MOSES
Four guineas.

CHARLES SURFACE
Four guineas! Gad's life, you don't bid me the price of his wig.—Mr. Premium, you have more respect for the woolsack; do let us knock his lordship down at fifteen.

SIR OLIVER
By all means.

CARELESS
Gone!

CHARLES SURFACE
And there are two brothers of his, William and Walter Blunt, Esquires, both members of Parliament, and noted speakers; and, what's very extraordinary, I believe, this is the first time they were ever bought or sold.

SIR OLIVER

That is very extraordinary, indeed! I'll take them at your own price, for the honour of Parliament.

CARELESS

Well said, little Premium! I'll knock them down at forty.

CHARLES SURFACE

Here's a jolly fellow—I don't know what relation, but he was mayor of Norwich: take him at eight pounds.

SIR OLIVER

No, no; six will do for the mayor.

CHARLES SURFACE

Come, make it guineas, and I'll throw you the two aldermen there into the bargain.

SIR OLIVER

They're mine.

CHARLES SURFACE

Careless, knock down the mayor and aldermen. But, plague on't! we shall be all day retailing in this manner; do let us deal wholesale: what say you, little Premium? Give me three hundred pounds for the rest of the family in the lump.

CARELESS

Ay, ay, that will be the best way.

SIR OLIVER

Well, well, anything to accommodate you; they are mine. But there is one portrait which you have always passed over.

CARELESS

What, that ill-looking little fellow over the settee?

SIR OLIVER

Yes, sir, I mean that; though I don't think him so ill-looking a little fellow, by any means.

CHARLES SURFACE

What, that? Oh; that's my uncle Oliver! 'Twas done before he went to India.

CARELESS

Your uncle Oliver! Gad, then you'll never be friends, Charles. That, now, to me, is as stern a looking rogue as ever I saw; an unforgiving eye, and a damned disinheriting countenance! an inveterate knave, depend on't. Don't you think so, little Premium?

SIR OLIVER

Upon my soul, sir, I do not; I think it is as honest a looking face as any in the room, dead or alive. But I suppose uncle Oliver goes with the rest of the lumber?

CHARLES SURFACE

No, hang it! I'll not part with poor Noll. The old fellow has been very good to me, and, egad, I'll keep his picture while I've a room to put it in.

SIR OLIVER

[*Aside.*] The rogue's my nephew after all!—[*Aloud.*] But, sir, I have somehow taken a fancy to that picture.

CHARLES SURFACE

I'm sorry for't, for you certainly will not have it. Oons, haven't you got enough of them?

SIR OLIVER

[*Aside*.] I forgive him everything!—[*Aloud*.] But, sir, when I take a whim in my head, I don't value money. I'll give you as much for that as for all the rest.

CHARLES SURFACE

Don't tease me, master broker; I tell you I'll not part with it, and there's an end of it.

SIR OLIVER

[*Aside*.] How like his father the dog is.—[*Aloud*.] Well, well, I have done.—[*Aside*.] I did not perceive it before, but I think I never saw such a striking resemblance.—[*Aloud*.] Here is a draught for your sum.

CHARLES SURFACE

Why, 'tis for eight hundred pounds!

SIR OLIVER

You will not let Sir Oliver go?

CHARLES SURFACE

Zounds! no! I tell you, once more.

SIR OLIVER

Then never mind the difference, we'll balance that another time. But give me your hand on the bargain; you are an honest fellow, Charles—I beg pardon, sir, for being so free.—Come, Moses.

CHARLES SURFACE

Egad, this is a whimsical old fellow!—But hark'ee, Premium, you'll prepare lodgings for these gentlemen.

SIR OLIVER

Yes, yes, I'll send for them in a day or two.

CHARLES SURFACE

But hold; do now send a genteel conveyance for them,
for, I assure you, they were most of them used to ride
in their own carriages.

SIR OLIVER

I will, I will—for all but Oliver.

CHARLES SURFACE

Ay, all but the little nabob.

SIR OLIVER

You're fixed on that?

CHARLES SURFACE

Peremptorily.

SIR OLIVER

[*Aside.*] A dear extravagant rogue!—[*Aloud.*] Good
day!—Come, Moses,—[*Aside.*] Let me hear now who
dares call him profligate!   [*Exit with* MOSES.

CARELESS

Why, this is the oddest genius of the sort I ever met
with!

CHARLES SURFACE

Egad, he's the prince of brokers, I think. I wonder
how the devil Moses got acquainted with so honest a
fellow.—Ha! here's Rowley.—Do, Careless, say I'll
join the company in a few moments.

CARELESS

I will—but don't let that old blockhead persuade you
to squander any of that money on old musty debts, or
any such nonsense; for tradesmen, Charles, are the
most exorbitant fellows.

CARELESS

CHARLES SURFACE
Very true, and paying them is only encouraging them.

CARELESS
Nothing else.

CHARLES SURFACE
Ay, ay, never fear.—[*Exit* CARELESS.] So! this was an odd old fellow, indeed. Let me see, two-thirds of these five hundred and thirty odd pounds are mine by right. 'Fore Heaven! I find one's ancestors are more valuable relations than I took them for!—Ladies and gentlemen, your most obedient and very grateful servant. [*Bows ceremoniously to the pictures.*

Enter ROWLEY

Ha! old Rowley! egad, you are just come in time to take leave of your old acquaintance.

ROWLEY
Yes, I heard they were a-going. But I wonder you can have such spirits under so many distresses.

CHARLES SURFACE
Why, there's the point! my distresses are so many, that I can't afford to part with my spirits; but I shall be rich and splenetic, all in good time. However, I suppose you are surprised that I am not more sorrowful at parting with so many near relations; to be sure, 'tis very affecting; but you see they never move a muscle, so why should I?

ROWLEY

There's no making you serious a moment.

CHARLES SURFACE

Yes, faith, I am so now. Here, my honest Rowley, here, get me this changed directly, and take a hundred pounds of it immediately to old Stanley.

ROWLEY

A hundred pounds! Consider only——

CHARLES SURFACE

Gad's life, don't talk about it! poor Stanley's wants are pressing, and, if you don't make haste, we shall have some one call that has a better right to the money.

ROWLEY

Ah! there's the point! I never will cease dunning you with the old proverb——

CHARLES SURFACE

Be just before you're generous.—Why, so I would if I could; but Justice is an old hobbling beldame, and I can't get her to keep pace with Generosity, for the soul of me.

ROWLEY

Yet, Charles, believe me, one hour's reflection——

CHARLES SURFACE

Ay, ay, it's very true; but, hark'ee, Rowley, while I have, by Heaven I'll give; so, damn your economy! and now for hazard.   [*Exeunt.*

SCENE TWO
Another room in the same

Enter SIR OLIVER SURFACE *and* MOSES

MOSES
Well, sir, I think, as Sir Peter said, you have seen
Mr. Charles in high glory; 'tis great pity he's so
extravagant.

SIR OLIVER
True, but he would not sell my picture.

MOSES
And loves wine and women so much.

SIR OLIVER
But he would not sell my picture.

MOSES
And games so deep.

SIR OLIVER
But he would not sell my picture. Oh, here's Rowley.

Enter ROWLEY

ROWLEY
So, Sir Oliver, I find you have made a purchase——

SIR OLIVER
Yes, yes, our young rake has parted with his ancestors
like old tapestry.

ROWLEY
And here has he commissioned me to re-deliver you
part of the purchase-money—I mean, though, in your
necessitous character of old Stanley.

267

MOSES

Ah! there is the pity of all: he is so damned charitable.

ROWLEY

And I left a hosier and two tailors in the hall, who, I'm sure, won't be paid, and this hundred would satisfy them.

SIR OLIVER

Well, well, I'll pay his debts, and his benevolence too. But now I am no more a broker, and you shall introduce me to the elder brother as old Stanley.

ROWLEY

Not yet awhile; Sir Peter, I know, means to call there about this time.

Enter TRIP

TRIP

Oh, gentlemen, I beg pardon for not showing you out; this way—Moses, a word.   [*Exit with* MOSES.

SIR OLIVER

There's a fellow for you! Would you believe it, that puppy intercepted the Jew on our coming, and wanted to raise money before he got to his master!

ROWLEY

Indeed.

SIR OLIVER

Yes, they are now planning an annuity business. Ah, Master Rowley, in my days servants were content with the follies of their masters, when they were worn a little threadbare; but now they have their vices, like their birthday clothes, with the gloss on.   [*Exeunt.*

SCENE THREE
A Library in JOSEPH SURFACE'S *House*

Enter JOSEPH SURFACE *and* SERVANT

JOSEPH SURFACE

No letter from Lady Teazle?

SERVANT

No, sir.

JOSEPH SURFACE

[*Aside.*] I am surprised she has not sent, if she is prevented from coming. Sir Peter certainly does not suspect me. Yet I wish I may not lose the heiress, through the scrape I have drawn myself into with the wife; however, Charles's imprudence and bad character are great points in my favour. [*Knocking without.*

SERVANT

Sir, I believe that must be Lady Teazle.

JOSEPH SURFACE

Hold! See whether it is or not, before you go to the door: I have a particular message for you if it should be my brother.

SERVANT

'Tis her ladyship, sir; she always leaves the chair at the milliner's in the next street.

JOSEPH SURFACE

Stay, stay: draw that screen before the window—that will do;—my opposite neighbour is a maiden lady of so curious a temper.—[SERVANT *draws the screen, and exit.*] I have a difficult hand to play in this affair. Lady Teazle has lately suspected my views on Maria; but she must by no means be let into that secret,—at least, till I have her more in my power.

Enter LADY TEAZLE

LADY TEAZLE

What sentiment in soliloquy now? Have you been very impatient? O Lud! don't pretend to look grave. I vow I couldn't come before.

JOSEPH SURFACE

O madam, punctuality is a species of constancy very unfashionable in a lady of quality.
[*Places chairs, and sits after* LADY TEAZLE *is seated.*

LADY TEAZLE

Upon my word, you ought to pity me. Do you know Sir Peter is grown so ill-natured to me of late, and so jealous of Charles too—that's the best of the story, isn't it?

JOSEPH SURFACE

I am glad my scandalous friends keep that up. [*Aside.*

LADY TEAZLE

I am sure I wish he would let Maria marry him, and then perhaps he would be convinced; don't you, Mr. Surface?

JOSEPH SURFACE

[*Aside.*] Indeed I do not.—[*Aloud.*] Oh, certainly I do! for then my dear Lady Teazle would also be convinced how wrong her suspicions were of my having any design on the silly girl.

LADY TEAZLE

Well, well, I'm inclined to believe you. But isn't it provoking, to have the most ill-natured things said of one? And there's my friend Lady Sneerwell has circulated I don't know how many scandalous tales of me, and all without any foundation, too; that's what vexes me.

JOSEPH SURFACE

Ay, madam, to be sure, that is the provoking circumstance—without foundation; yes, yes, there's the mortification, indeed; for, when a scandalous story is believed against one, there certainly is no comfort like the consciousness of having deserved it.

LADY TEAZLE

No, to be sure, then I'd forgive their malice; but to attack me, who am really so innocent, and who never say an ill-natured thing of anybody—that is, of any friend; and then Sir Peter, too, to have him so peevish, and so suspicious, when I know the integrity of my own heart—indeed 'tis monstrous!

JOSEPH SURFACE

But, my dear Lady Teazle, 'tis your own fault if you suffer it. When a husband entertains a groundless suspicion of his wife, and withdraws his confidence from her, the original compact is broken, and she owes it to the honour of her sex to endeavour to outwit him.

LADY TEAZLE

Indeed! So that, if he suspects me without cause, it follows, that the best way of curing his jealousy is to give him reason for't?

JOSEPH SURFACE

Undoubtedly—for your husband should never be deceived in you: and in that case it becomes you to be frail in compliment to his discernment.

LADY TEAZLE

To be sure, what you say is very reasonable, and when the consciousness of my innocence——

JOSEPH SURFACE

Ah, my dear madam, there is the great mistake; 'tis this very conscious innocence that is of the greatest prejudice to you. What is it makes you negligent of forms, and careless of the world's opinion? why, the consciousness of your own innocence. What makes you thoughtless in your conduct, and apt to run into a thousand little imprudences? why, the consciousness of your own innocence. What makes you impatient of Sir Peter's temper, and outrageous at his suspicions? why, the consciousness of your innocence.

LADY TEAZLE

'Tis very true!

JOSEPH SURFACE

Now, my dear Lady Teazle, if you would but once make a trifling *faux pas*, you can't conceive how cautious you would grow, and how ready to humour and agree with your husband.

LADY TEAZLE

Do you think so?

JOSEPH SURFACE

Oh, I'm sure on't; and then you would find all scandal would cease at once, for—in short, your character at present is like a person in a plethora, absolutely dying from too much health.

LADY TEAZLE
So, so; then I perceive your prescription is, that I must sin in my own defence, and part with my virtue to preserve my reputation?

JOSEPH SURFACE
Exactly so, upon my credit, ma'am.

LADY TEAZLE
Well, certainly this is the oddest doctrine, and the newest receipt for avoiding calumny?

JOSEPH SURFACE
An infallible one, believe me. Prudence, like experience, must be paid for.

LADY TEAZLE
Why, if my understanding were once convinced——

JOSEPH SURFACE
Oh, certainly, madam, your understanding should be convinced. Yes, yes—Heaven forbid I should persuade you to do anything you thought wrong. No, no, I have too much honour to desire it.

LADY TEAZLE
Don't you think we may as well leave honour out of the argument?   [*Rises.*

JOSEPH SURFACE
Ah, the ill effects of your country education, I see, still remain with you.

273

LADY TEAZLE

I doubt they do, indeed; and I will fairly own to you, that if I could be persuaded to do wrong, it would be by Sir Peter's ill-usage sooner than your honourable logic, after all.

JOSEPH SURFACE

Then, by this hand, which he is unworthy of——
[*Taking her hand.*

Re-enter SERVANT

'Sdeath, you blockhead—what do you want?

SERVANT

I beg your pardon, sir, but I thought you would not choose Sir Peter to come up without announcing him.

JOSEPH SURFACE

Sir Peter!—Oons—the devil!

LADY TEAZLE

Sir Peter! O Lud! I'm ruined! I'm ruined!

SERVANT

Sir, 'twasn't I let him in.

LADY TEAZLE

Oh! I'm quite undone! What will become of me? Now, Mr. Logic—Oh! mercy, sir, he's on the stairs— I'll get behind here—and if ever I'm so imprudent again—— [*Goes behind the screen.*

JOSEPH SURFACE

Give me that book.
[*Sits down.* SERVANT *pretends to adjust his chair.*

Enter SIR PETER TEAZLE

SIR PETER

Ay, ever improving himself. Mr. Surface, Mr. Surface——   [*Pats* JOSEPH *on the shoulder.*

JOSEPH SURFACE

Oh, my dear Sir Peter, I beg your pardon. [*Gaping, throws away the book.*] I have been dozing over a stupid book. Well, I am much obliged to you for this call. You haven't been here, I believe, since I fitted up this room. Books, you know, are the only things I am a coxcomb in.

SIR PETER

'Tis very neat indeed. Well, well, that's proper; and you can make even your screen a source of knowledge —hung, I perceive, with maps.

JOSEPH SURFACE

Oh, yes, I find great use in that screen.

SIR PETER

I dare say you must, certainly, when you want to find anything in a hurry.

JOSEPH SURFACE

Ay, or to hide anything in a hurry either.   [*Aside.*

SIR PETER

Well, I have a little private business——

JOSEPH SURFACE

You need not stay.   [*To* SERVANT.

SERVANT

No, sir.   [*Exit.*

JOSEPH SURFACE
Here's a chair, Sir Peter—I beg——

SIR PETER
Well, now we are alone, there is a subject, my dear friend, on which I wish to unburden my mind to you —a point of the greatest moment to my peace; in short, my good friend, Lady Teazle's conduct of late has made me very unhappy.

JOSEPH SURFACE
Indeed! I am very sorry to hear it.

SIR PETER
Yes, 'tis but too plain she has not the least regard for me; but, what's worse, I have pretty good authority to suppose she has formed an attachment to another.

JOSEPH SURFACE
Indeed! you astonish me!

SIR PETER
Yes! and, between ourselves, I think I've discovered the person.

JOSEPH SURFACE
How! you alarm me exceedingly.

SIR PETER
Ay, my dear friend, I knew you would sympathize with me!

JOSEPH SURFACE
Yes, believe me, Sir Peter, such a discovery would hurt me just as much as it would you.

SIR PETER

I am convinced of it. Ah! it is a happiness to have a friend whom we can trust even with one's family secrets. But have you no guess who I mean?

JOSEPH SURFACE

I haven't the most distant idea. It can't be Sir Benjamin Backbite!

SIR PETER

Oh, no! What say you to Charles?

JOSEPH SURFACE

My brother! impossible!

SIR PETER

Oh, my dear friend, the goodness of your own heart misleads you. You judge of others by yourself.

JOSEPH SURFACE

Certainly, Sir Peter, the heart that is conscious of its own integrity is ever slow to credit another's treachery.

SIR PETER

True; but your brother has no sentiment—you never hear him talk so.

JOSEPH SURFACE

Yet I can't but think Lady Teazle herself has too much principle.

SIR PETER

Ay; but what is principle against the flattery of a handsome, lively young fellow?

JOSEPH SURFACE

That's very true.

SIR PETER

And then, you know, the difference of our ages makes it very improbable that she should have any great affection for me; and if she were to be frail, and I were to make it public, why the town would only laugh at me, the foolish old bachelor, who had married a girl.

JOSEPH SURFACE

That's true, to be sure—they would laugh.

SIR PETER

Laugh! ay, and make ballads, and paragraphs, and the devil knows what of me.

JOSEPH SURFACE

No, you must never make it public.

SIR PETER

But then again—that the nephew of my old friend, Sir Oliver, should be the person to attempt such a wrong, hurts me more nearly.

JOSEPH SURFACE

Ay, there's the point. When ingratitude barbs the dart of injury, the wound has double danger in it.

SIR PETER

Ay—I, that was, in a manner, left his guardian: in whose house he had been so often entertained; who never in my life denied him—my advice!

JOSEPH SURFACE

Oh, 'tis not to be credited! There may be a man capable of such baseness, to be sure; but, for my part, till you can give me positive proofs, I cannot but doubt it. However, if it should be proved on him, he is no longer a brother of mine—I disclaim kindred with him: for the man who can break the laws of hospitality, and tempt the wife of his friend, deserves to be branded as the pest of society.

SIR PETER

What a difference there is between you! What noble sentiments!

JOSEPH SURFACE

Yet I cannot suspect Lady Teazle's honour.

SIR PETER

I am sure I wish to think well of her, and to remove all ground of quarrel between us. She has lately reproached me more than once with having made no settlement on her; and, in our last quarrel, she almost hinted that she should not break her heart if I was dead. Now, as we seem to differ in our ideas of expense, I have resolved she shall have her own way, and be her own mistress in that respect for the future; and, if I were to die, she will find I have not been inattentive to her interest while living. Here, my friend, are the drafts of two deeds, which I wish to have your opinion on. By one, she will enjoy eight hundred a year independent while I live; and, by the other, the bulk of my fortune at my death.

JOSEPH SURFACE

This conduct, Sir Peter, is indeed truly generous.— [*Aside.*] I wish it may not corrupt my pupil.

SIR PETER

Yes, I am determined she shall have no cause to complain, though I would not have her acquainted with the latter instance of my affection yet awhile.

JOSEPH SURFACE

Nor I, if I could help it.   [*Aside.*

SIR PETER

And now, my dear friend, if you please, we will talk over the situation of your hopes with Maria.

JOSEPH SURFACE

[*Softly.*] Oh, no, Sir Peter; another time, if you please.

SIR PETER

I am sensibly chagrined at the little progress you seem to make in her affections.

JOSEPH SURFACE

[*Softly.*] I beg you will not mention it. What are my disappointments when your happiness is in debate!—[*Aside.*] 'Sdeath, I shall be ruined every way!

SIR PETER

And though you are averse to my acquainting Lady Teazle with your passion, I'm sure she's not your enemy in the affair.

JOSEPH SURFACE

Pray, Sir Peter, now oblige me. I am really too much affected by the subject we have been speaking of to bestow a thought on my own concerns. The man who is entrusted with his friend's distresses can never——

Re-enter SERVANT

Well, sir?

SERVANT

Your brother, sir, is speaking to a gentleman in the street, and says he knows you are within.

JOSEPH SURFACE

JOSEPH SURFACE

'Sdeath, blockhead, I'm not within—I'm out for the day.

SIR PETER

Stay—hold—a thought has struck me:—you shall be at home.

JOSEPH SURFACE

Well, well, let him up.—[*Exit* SERVANT.] He'll interrupt Sir Peter, however.   [*Aside.*

SIR PETER

Now, my good friend, oblige me, I entreat you. Before Charles comes, let me conceal myself somewhere, then do you tax him on the point we have been talking, and his answer may satisfy me at once.

JOSEPH SURFACE

Oh, fie, Sir Peter! would you have me join in so mean a trick?—to trepan my brother too?

SIR PETER

Nay, you tell me you are sure he is innocent; if so, you do him the greatest service by giving him an opportunity to clear himself, and you will set my heart at rest. Come, you shall not refuse me: [*Going up*] here, behind the screen will be—Hey! what the devil! there seems to be one listener here already— I'll swear I saw a petticoat!

JOSEPH SURFACE

Ha! ha! ha! Well, this is ridiculous enough. I'll tell you, Sir Peter, though I hold a man of intrigue to be a most despicable character, yet you know, it does not follow that one is to be an absolute Joseph either!

Hark'ee, 'tis a little French milliner, a silly rogue that plagues me; and having some character to lose, on your coming, sir, she ran behind the screen.

SIR PETER

Ah, a rogue—— But, egad, she has overheard all I have been saying of my wife.

JOSEPH SURFACE

Oh, 'twill never go any farther, you may depend upon it!

SIR PETER

No! then, faith, let her hear it out.—Here's a closet will do as well.

JOSEPH SURFACE

Well, go in there.

SIR PETER

Sly rogue! sly rogue!   [*Goes into the closet.*

JOSEPH SURFACE

A narrow escape, indeed! and a curious situation I'm in, to part man and wife in this manner.

LADY TEAZLE

[*Peeping.*] Couldn't I steal off?

JOSEPH SURFACE

Keep close, my angel!

SIR PETER

[*Peeping.*] Joseph, tax him home.

JOSEPH SURFACE

Back, my dear friend!

LADY TEAZLE

[*Peeping.*] Couldn't you lock Sir Peter in?

JOSEPH SURFACE

Be still, my life!

SIR PETER

[*Peeping.*] You're sure the little milliner won't blab?

JOSEPH SURFACE

In, in, my dear Sir Peter!—'Fore Gad, I wish I had a key to the door.

Enter CHARLES SURFACE

CHARLES SURFACE

Holla! brother, what has been the matter? Your fellow would not let me up at first. What! have you had a Jew or a wench with you?

JOSEPH SURFACE

Neither, brother, I assure you.

CHARLES SURFACE

But what has made Sir Peter steal off? I thought he had been with you.

JOSEPH SURFACE

He was, brother; but, hearing you were coming, he did not choose to stay.

CHARLES SURFACE

What! was the old gentleman afraid I wanted to borrow money of him!

JOSEPH SURFACE

No, sir: but I am sorry to find, Charles, you have lately given that worthy man grounds for great uneasiness.

CHARLES SURFACE

Yes, they tell me I do that to a great many worthy men. But how so, pray?

JOSEPH SURFACE

To be plain with you, brother, he thinks you are endeavouring to gain Lady Teazle's affections from him.

CHARLES SURFACE

Who, I? O Lud! not I, upon my word.—Ha! ha! ha! ha! so the old fellow has found out that he has got a young wife, has he?—or, what is worse, Lady Teazle has found out she has an old husband?

JOSEPH SURFACE

This is no subject to jest on, brother. He who can laugh——

CHARLES SURFACE

True, true, as you were going to say—then, seriously, I never had the least idea of what you charge me with, upon my honour.

JOSEPH SURFACE

Well, it will give Sir Peter great satisfaction to hear this. [*Raising his voice.*

CHARLES SURFACE

To be sure, I once thought the lady seemed to have taken a fancy to me; but, upon my soul, I never gave her the least encouragement. Besides, you know my attachment to Maria.

JOSEPH SURFACE

But sure, brother, even if Lady Teazle had betrayed the fondest partiality for you——

CHARLES SURFACE
Why, look'ee, Joseph, I hope I shall never deliberately
do a dishonourable action; but if a pretty woman was
purposely to throw herself in my way—and that
pretty woman married to a man old enough to be her
father——

JOSEPH SURFACE
Well!

CHARLES SURFACE
Why, I believe I should be obliged to borrow a little
of your morality, that's all. But, brother, do you
know now that you surprise me exceedingly, by
naming me with Lady Teazle; for i'faith, I always
understood you were her favourite.

JOSEPH SURFACE
Oh, for shame, Charles! This retort is foolish.

CHARLES SURFACE
Nay, I swear I have seen you exchange such signifi-
cant glances——

JOSEPH SURFACE
Nay, nay, sir, this is no jest.

CHARLES SURFACE
Egad, I'm serious! Don't you remember one day,
when I called here——

JOSEPH SURFACE
Nay, pr'ythee, Charles——

CHARLES SURFACE
And found you together——

JOSEPH SURFACE
Zounds, sir, I insist——

CHARLES SURFACE

And another time, when your servant——

JOSEPH SURFACE

Brother, brother, a word with you!—[*Aside.*] Gad, I must stop him.

CHARLES SURFACE

Informed, I say, that——

JOSEPH SURFACE

Hush! I beg your pardon, but Sir Peter has overheard all we have been saying. I knew you would clear yourself, or I should not have consented.

CHARLES SURFACE

How, Sir Peter! Where is he?

JOSEPH SURFACE

Softly, there! [*Points to the closet.*

CHARLES SURFACE

Oh, 'fore Heaven, I'll have him out. Sir Peter, come forth!

JOSEPH SURFACE

No, no——

CHARLES SURFACE

I say, Sir Peter, come into court.—[*Pulls in* SIR PETER.] What! my old guardian!—What!—turn inquisitor, and take evidence, incog.? Oh, fie! Oh, fie!

SIR PETER

Give me your hand, Charles—I believe I have suspected you wrongfully; but you mustn't be angry with Joseph—'twas my plan!

CHARLES SURFACE

Indeed!

SIR PETER

But I acquit you. I promise you I don't think near so ill of you as I did. What I have heard has given me great satisfaction.

CHARLES SURFACE

Egad, then, 'twas lucky you didn't hear any more. Wasn't it, Joseph?

SIR PETER

Ah! you would have retorted on him.

CHARLES SURFACE

Ah, ay, that was a joke.

SIR PETER

Yes, yes, I know his honour too well.

CHARLES SURFACE

But you might as well have suspected him as me in this matter, for all that. Mightn't he, Joseph?

SIR PETER

Well, well, I believe you.

JOSEPH SURFACE

Would they were both out of the room!   [*Aside.*

SIR PETER

And in future, perhaps, we may not be such strangers.

Re-enter SERVANT *and whispers* JOSEPH SURFACE

SERVANT

Lady Sneerwell is below, and says she will come up.

JOSEPH SURFACE

Gentlemen, I beg pardon—I must wait on you downstairs; here's a person come on particular business.

CHARLES SURFACE

Well, you can see him in another room. Sir Peter and I have not met a long time, and I have something to say to him.

JOSEPH SURFACE

[*Aside.*] They must not be left together.—[*Aloud.*] I'll send Lady Sneerwell away, and return directly.— [*Aside to* SIR PETER.] Sir Peter, not a word of the French milliner.

SIR PETER

[*Aside to* JOSEPH SURFACE.] I! not for the world!— [*Exit* JOSEPH SURFACE.] Ah, Charles, if you associated more with your brother, one might indeed hope for your reformation. He is a man of sentiment. Well, there is nothing in the world so noble as a man of sentiment.

CHARLES SURFACE

Psha! he is too moral by half; and so apprehensive of his good name, as he calls it, that I suppose he would as soon let a priest into his house as a wench.

SIR PETER

No, no,—come, come,—you wrong him. No, no, Joseph is no rake, but he is no such saint either, in that respect.—[*Aside.*] I have a great mind to tell him —we should have such a laugh at Joseph.

CHARLES SURFACE

Oh, hang him! he's a very anchorite, a young hermit!

SIR PETER TEAZLE

SIR PETER

Hark'ee—you must not abuse him: he may chance to hear of it again, I promise you.

CHARLES SURFACE

Why, you won't tell him?

SIR PETER

No—but—this way.—[*Aside.*] Egad, I'll tell him. [*Aloud.*] Hark'ee, have you a mind to have a good laugh at Joseph?

CHARLES SURFACE

I should like it of all things.

SIR PETER

Then, i'faith, we will! I'll be quit with him for dis-covering me. He had a girl with him when I called.

[*Whispers.*

CHARLES SURFACE

What! Joseph? you jest.

SIR PETER

Hush!—a little French milliner—and the best of the jest is—she's in the room now.

CHARLES SURFACE

The devil she is!

SIR PETER

Hush! I tell you.   [*Points to the screen.*

CHARLES SURFACE

Behind the screen! Odds life, let's unveil her!

SIR PETER

No, no, he's coming:—you shan't, indeed!

CHARLES SURFACE

Oh, egad, we'll have a peep at the little milliner!

2A   289

SIR PETER
  Not for the world!—Joseph will never forgive me.

CHARLES SURFACE
  I'll stand by you——

SIR PETER
  Odds, here he is!

[CHARLES SURFACE *throws down the screen.*
  Re-enter JOSEPH SURFACE

CHARLES SURFACE
  Lady Teazle, by all that's wonderful!

SIR PETER
  Lady Teazle, by all that's damnable!

CHARLES SURFACE
  Sir Peter, this is one of the smartest French milliners
  I ever saw. Egad, you seem all to have been diverting
  yourselves here at hide and seek, and I don't see who
  is out of the secret. Shall I beg your ladyship to
  inform me? Not a word!—Brother, will you be
  pleased to explain this matter? What! is Morality
  dumb too?—Sir Peter, though I found you in the
  dark, perhaps you are not so now! All mute! Well—
  though I can make nothing of the affair, I suppose
  you perfectly understand one another; so I'll leave
  you to yourselves.—[*Going.*] Brother, I'm sorry to
  find you have given that worthy man grounds for so
  much uneasiness.—Sir Peter! there's nothing in the
  world so noble as a man of sentiment!   [*Exit.*

JOSEPH SURFACE

Sir Peter—notwithstanding—I confess—that appearances are against me—if you will afford me your patience—I make no doubt—but I shall explain everything to your satisfaction.

SIR PETER

If you please, sir.

JOSEPH SURFACE

The fact is, sir, that Lady Teazle, knowing my pretensions to your ward Maria—I say, sir, Lady Teazle, being apprehensive of the jealousy of your temper—and knowing my friendship to the family—she, sir, I say—called here—in order that—I might explain these pretensions—but on your coming—being apprehensive—as I said—of your jealousy—she withdrew—and this, you may depend on it, is the whole truth of the matter.

SIR PETER

A very clear account, upon my word; and I dare swear the lady will vouch for every article of it.

LADY TEAZLE

For not one word of it, Sir Peter!

SIR PETER

How! don't you think it worth while to agree in the lie?

LADY TEAZLE

There is not one syllable of truth in what that gentleman has told you.

SIR PETER

I believe you, upon my soul, ma'am!

JOSEPH SURFACE

[*Aside to* LADY TEAZLE.] 'Sdeath, madam, will you betray me?

LADY TEAZLE

Good Mr. Hypocrite, by your leave, I'll speak for myself.

SIR PETER

Ay, let her alone, sir; you'll find she'll make out a better story than you, without prompting.

LADY TEAZLE

Hear me, Sir Peter!—I came here on no matter relating to your ward, and even ignorant of this gentleman's pretensions to her. But I came, seduced by his insidious arguments, at least to listen to his pretended passion, if not to sacrifice your honour to his baseness.

SIR PETER

Now, I believe, the truth is coming, indeed!

JOSEPH SURFACE

The woman's mad!

LADY TEAZLE

No, sir; she has recovered her senses, and your own arts have furnished her with the means.—Sir Peter, I do not expect you to credit me—but the tenderness you expressed for me, when I am sure you could not think I was a witness to it, has penetrated so to my heart, that had I left the place without the shame of this discovery, my future life should have spoken the sincerity of my gratitude. As for that smooth-tongued hypocrite, who would have seduced the wife of his too credulous friend, while he affected honourable addresses to his ward—I behold him now in a light so truly despicable, that I shall never again respect myself for having listened to him. [*Exit.*

JOSEPH SURFACE
Notwithstanding all this, Sir Peter, Heaven knows——

SIR PETER
That you are a villain! and so I leave you to your conscience.

JOSEPH SURFACE
You are too rash, Sir Peter; you shall hear me. The man who shuts out conviction by refusing to——
[*Exeunt* SIR PETER *and* JOSEPH SURFACE, *talking.*

ACT FIVE

SCENE ONE

The Library in JOSEPH SURFACE'S *House*

Enter JOSEPH SURFACE *and* SERVANT

JOSEPH SURFACE

Mr. Stanley! and why should you think I would see him? you must know he comes to ask something.

SERVANT

Sir, I should not have let him in, but that Mr. Rowley came to the door with him.

JOSEPH SURFACE

Psha! blockhead! to suppose that I should now be in a temper to receive visits from poor relations!—Well, why don't you show the fellow up?

SERVANT

I will, sir.—Why, sir, it was not my fault that Sir Peter discovered my lady——

JOSEPH SURFACE

Go, fool!—[*Exit* SERVANT.] Sure Fortune never played a man of my policy such a trick before! My character with Sir Peter, my hopes with Maria, destroyed in a moment! I'm in a rare humour to listen to other people's distresses! I shan't be able to bestow even a benevolent sentiment on Stanley.— So! here he comes, and Rowley with him. I must try to recover myself, and put a little charity into my face, however.   [*Exit.*

Enter SIR OLIVER SURFACE *and* ROWLEY

SIR OLIVER

What! does he avoid us? That was he, was it not?

ROWLEY

It was, sir. But I doubt you are come a little too abruptly. His nerves are so weak, that the sight of a poor relation may be too much for him. I should have gone first to break it to him.

SIR OLIVER

Oh, plague of his nerves! Yet this is he whom Sir Peter extols as a man of the most benevolent way of thinking!

ROWLEY

As to his way of thinking, I cannot pretend to decide; for, to do him justice, he appears to have as much speculative benevolence as any private gentleman in the kingdom, though he is seldom so sensual as to indulge himself in the exercise of it.

SIR OLIVER

Yet he has a string of charitable sentiments at his fingers' ends.

ROWLEY

Or, rather, at his tongue's end, Sir Oliver; for I believe there is no sentiment he has such faith in as that *Charity begins at home.*

SIR OLIVER

And his, I presume, is of that domestic sort which never stirs abroad at all.

ROWLEY

I doubt you'll find it so;—but he's coming. I mustn't seem to interrupt you; and you know, immediately as you leave him, I come in to announce your arrival in your real character.

SIR OLIVER

True; and afterwards you'll meet me at Sir Peter's.

ROWLEY

Without losing a moment.   [*Exit.*

SIR OLIVER

I don't like the complaisance of his features.

Re-enter JOSEPH SURFACE

JOSEPH SURFACE

Sir, I beg you ten thousand pardons for keeping you a moment waiting.—Mr. Stanley, I presume.

SIR OLIVER

At your service.

JOSEPH SURFACE

Sir, I beg you will do me the honour to sit down— I entreat you, sir.

SIR OLIVER

Dear sir—there's no occasion.—[*Aside.*] Too civil by half!

JOSEPH SURFACE

I have not the pleasure of knowing you, Mr. Stanley; but I am extremely happy to see you look so well. You were nearly related to my mother, I think, Mr. Stanley?

SIR OLIVER

I was, sir; so nearly that my present poverty, I fear, may do discredit to her wealthy children, else I should not have presumed to trouble you.

JOSEPH SURFACE

Dear sir, there needs no apology: he that is in distress, though a stranger, has a right to claim kindred with the wealthy. I am sure I wish I was one of that class, and had it in my power to offer you even a small relief.

SIR OLIVER

If your uncle, Sir Oliver, were here, I should have a friend.

JOSEPH SURFACE

I wish he was, sir, with all my heart: you should not want an advocate with him, believe me, sir.

SIR OLIVER

I should not need one—my distresses would recommend me. But I imagined his bounty would enable you to become the agent of his charity.

JOSEPH SURFACE

My dear sir, you were strangely misinformed. Sir Oliver is a worthy man, a very worthy man; but avarice, Mr. Stanley, is the vice of age. I will tell you, my good sir, in confidence, what he has done for me has been a mere nothing; though people, I know, have thought otherwise, and, for my part, I never chose to contradict the report.

SIR OLIVER

What! has he never transmitted you bullion—rupees —pagodas?

JOSEPH SURFACE

Oh, dear sir, nothing of the kind! No, no; a few presents now and then—china, shawls, congou tea, avadavats, and Indian crackers—little more, believe me.

SIR OLIVER

Here's gratitude for twelve thousand pounds!— Avadavats and Indian crackers!   [*Aside.*

JOSEPH SURFACE

Then, my dear sir, you have heard, I doubt not, of the extravagance of my brother; there are very few would credit what I have done for that unfortunate young man.

SIR OLIVER

Not I, for one!   [*Aside.*

JOSEPH SURFACE

The sums I have lent him! Indeed I have been exceedingly to blame; it was an amiable weakness; however, I don't pretend to defend it—and now I feel it doubly culpable, since it has deprived me of the pleasure of serving you, Mr. Stanley, as my heart dictates.

SIR OLIVER

[*Aside.*] Dissembler!—[*Aloud.*] Then, sir, you can't assist me?

JOSEPH SURFACE

At present, it grieves me to say, I cannot; but, whenever I have the ability, you may depend upon hearing from me.

SIR OLIVER

I am extremely sorry——

JOSEPH SURFACE

Not more than I, believe me; to pity, without the power to relieve, is still more painful than to ask and be denied.

SIR OLIVER

Kind sir, your most obedient humble servant.

JOSEPH SURFACE

You leave me deeply affected, Mr. Stanley.— William, be ready to open the door.

[*Calls to* SERVANT.

SIR OLIVER

O, dear sir, no ceremony.

JOSEPH SURFACE

Your very obedient.

SIR OLIVER

Your most obsequious.

JOSEPH SURFACE

You may depend upon hearing from me, whenever I can be of service.

SIR OLIVER

Sweet sir, you are too good.

JOSEPH SURFACE

In the meantime I wish you health and spirits.

SIR OLIVER

Your ever grateful and perpetual humble servant.

JOSEPH SURFACE

Sir, yours as sincerely.

SIR OLIVER

Charles!—you are my heir.   [*Exit.*

JOSEPH SURFACE

This is one bad effect of a good character; it invites application from the unfortunate, and there needs no small degree of address to gain the reputation of benevolence without incurring the expense. The silver ore of pure charity is an expensive article in the catalogue of a man's good qualities; whereas the sentimental French plate I use instead of it makes just as good a show, and pays no tax.

Re-enter ROWLEY

ROWLEY

Mr. Surface, your servant: I was apprehensive of interrupting you, though my business demands immediate attention, as this note will inform you.

JOSEPH SURFACE

Always happy to see Mr. Rowley.—[*Aside. Reads the letter.*] Sir Oliver Surface!—My uncle arrived!

ROWLEY

He is, indeed: we have just parted—quite well, after a speedy voyage, and impatient to embrace his worthy nephew.

JOSEPH SURFACE

I am astonished!—William! stop Mr. Stanley, if he's not gone.   [*Calls to* SERVANT.

ROWLEY

Oh! he's out of reach, I believe.

JOSEPH SURFACE

Why did you not let me know this when you came in together?

ROWLEY

I thought you had particular business. But I must be gone to inform your brother, and appoint him here to meet your uncle. He will be with you in a quarter of an hour.

JOSEPH SURFACE

So he says. Well, I am strangely overjoyed at his coming.—[*Aside.*] Never, to be sure, was anything so damned unlucky!

ROWLEY

You will be delighted to see how well he looks.

JOSEPH SURFACE

Oh! I'm overjoyed to hear it.—[*Aside.*]—Just at this time!

ROWLEY

I'll tell him how impatiently you expect him.

JOSEPH SURFACE

Do, do; pray give my best duty and affection. Indeed, I cannot express the sensations I feel at the thought of seeing him.—[*Exit* ROWLEY.] Certainly his coming just at this time is the cruellest piece of ill fortune.

[*Exit.*

SCENE TWO

A Room in SIR PETER TEAZLE'S *House*

Enter MRS. CANDOUR *and* MAID

MAID

Indeed, ma'am, my lady will see nobody at present.

MRS. CANDOUR

Did you tell her it was her friend Mrs. Candour?

MAID

Yes, ma'am; but she begs you will excuse her.

MRS. CANDOUR

Do go again; I shall be glad to see her, if it be only for a moment, for I am sure she must be in great distress. —[*Exit* MAID.] Dear heart, how provoking! I'm not mistress of half the circumstances! We shall have the whole affair in the newspapers, with the names of the parties at length, before I have dropped the story at a dozen houses.

Enter SIR BENJAMIN BACKBITE

Oh, dear Sir Benjamin! you have heard, I suppose——

SIR BENJAMIN

Of Lady Teazle and Mr. Surface——

MRS. CANDOUR

And Sir Peter's discovery——

SIR BENJAMIN

Oh, the strangest piece of business, to be sure!

MRS. CANDOUR

Well, I never was so surprised in my life. I am so sorry for all parties, indeed.

SIR BENJAMIN

Now, I don't pity Sir Peter at all: he was so extravagantly partial to Mr. Surface.

MRS. CANDOUR

Mr. Surface! Why, 'twas with Charles Lady Teazle was detected.

SIR BENJAMIN

No, no, I tell you: Mr. Surface is the gallant.

MRS. CANDOUR

No such thing! Charles is the man. 'Twas Mr. Surface brought Sir Peter on purpose to discover them.

SIR BENJAMIN

I tell you I had it from one——

MRS. CANDOUR

And I have it from one——

SIR BENJAMIN

Who had it from one, who had it——

MRS. CANDOUR

From one immediately——But here comes Lady Sneerwell; perhaps she knows the whole affair.

Enter LADY SNEERWELL

LADY SNEERWELL

So, my dear Mrs. Candour, here's a sad affair of our friend Lady Teazle!

MRS. CANDOUR

Ay, my dear friend, who would have thought——

LADY SNEERWELL

Well, there is no trusting to appearances; though indeed, she was always too lively for me.

MRS. CANDOUR

To be sure, her manners were a little too free; but then she was so young!

LADY SNEERWELL

And had, indeed, some good qualities.

MRS. CANDOUR

So she had, indeed. But have you heard the particulars?

LADY SNEERWELL

No; but everybody says that Mr. Surface——

SIR BENJAMIN

Ay, there; I told you Mr. Surface was the man.

MRS. CANDOUR

No, no: indeed the assignation was with Charles.

LADY SNEERWELL

With Charles! You alarm me, Mrs. Candour.

MRS. CANDOUR

Yes, yes: he was the lover. Mr. Surface, to do him justice, was only the informer.

SIR BENJAMIN

Well, I'll not dispute with you, Mrs. Candour; but, be it which it may, I hope that Sir Peter's wound will not——

MRS. CANDOUR

Sir Peter's wound! Oh, mercy! I didn't hear a word of their fighting.

LADY SNEERWELL

Nor I, a syllable.

SIR BENJAMIN

No! what, no mention of the duel?

MRS. CANDOUR

Not a word.

SIR BENJAMIN

Oh, yes: they fought before they left the room.

LADY SNEERWELL

Pray, let us hear.

Sir Benjamin Backbite

MRS. CANDOUR

Ay, do oblige us with the duel.

SIR BENJAMIN

'*Sir*,' says Sir Peter, immediately after the discovery, '*you are a most ungrateful fellow.*'

MRS. CANDOUR

Ay, to Charles——

SIR BENJAMIN

No, no—to Mr. Surface—'*a most ungrateful fellow; and old as I am, sir,*' says he, '*I insist on immediate satisfaction.*'

MRS. CANDOUR

Ay, that must have been to Charles; for 'tis very unlikely Mr. Surface should fight in his own house.

SIR BENJAMIN

'Gad's life, ma'am, not at all—'*giving me immediate satisfaction.*'—On this, ma'am, Lady Teazle, seeing Sir Peter in such danger, ran out of the room in strong hysterics, and Charles after her, calling out for hartshorn and water; then, madam, they began to fight with swords——

Enter CRABTREE

CRABTREE

With pistols, nephew—pistols! I have it from undoubted authority.

MRS. CANDOUR

Oh, Mr. Crabtree, then it is all true!

CRABTREE

Too true, indeed, madam, and Sir Peter is dangerously wounded——

SIR BENJAMIN
By a thrust in second quite through his left side——

CRABTREE
By a bullet lodged in the thorax.

MRS. CANDOUR
Mercy on me! Poor Sir Peter!

CRABTREE
Yes, madam; though Charles would have avoided the matter, if he could.

MRS. CANDOUR
I knew Charles was the person.

SIR BENJAMIN
My uncle, I see, knows nothing of the matter.

CRABTREE
But Sir Peter taxed him with the basest ingratitude——

SIR BENJAMIN
That I told you, you know——

CRABTREE
Do, nephew, let me speak!—and insisted on immediate——

SIR BENJAMIN
Just as I said——

CRABTREE
Odds life, nephew, allow others to know something too! A pair of pistols lay on the bureau (for Mr. Surface, it seems, had come home the night before late from Salthill, where he had been to see the Montem with a friend, who has a son at Eton), so, unluckily, the pistols were left charged.

SIR BENJAMIN
   I heard nothing of this.

CRABTREE
   Sir Peter forced Charles to take one, and they fired, it seems, pretty nearly together. Charles's shot took effect, as I tell you, and Sir Peter's missed; but, what is very extraordinary, the ball struck against a little bronze Shakspeare that stood over the fireplace, grazed out of the window at a right angle, and wounded the postman, who was just coming to the door with a double letter from Northamptonshire.

SIR BENJAMIN
   My uncle's account is more circumstantial, I confess; but I believe mine is the true one, for all that.

LADY SNEERWELL
   [*Aside.*] I am more interested in this affair than they imagine, and must have better information.   [*Exit.*

SIR BENJAMIN
   Ah! Lady Sneerwell's alarm is very easily accounted for.

CRABTREE
   Yes, yes, they certainly do say—but that's neither here nor there.

MRS. CANDOUR
   But, pray, where is Sir Peter at present?

CRABTREE
   Oh! they brought him home, and he is now in the house, though the servants are ordered to deny him.

MRS. CANDOUR

I believe so, and Lady Teazle, I suppose, attending him.

CRABTREE

Yes, yes; and I saw one of the faculty enter just before me.

SIR BENJAMIN

Hey! who comes here?

CRABTREE

Oh, this is he: the physician, depend on't.

MRS. CANDOUR

Oh, certainly! it must be the physician; and now we shall know.

Enter SIR OLIVER SURFACE

CRABTREE

Well, doctor, what hopes?

MRS. CANDOUR

Ay, doctor, how's your patient?

SIR BENJAMIN

Now, doctor, isn't it a wound with a small-sword?

CRABTREE

A bullet lodged in the thorax, for a hundred!

SIR OLIVER

Doctor! a wound with a small-sword! and a bullet in the thorax?—Oons! are you mad, good people?

SIR BENJAMIN

Perhaps, sir, you are not a doctor?

SIR OLIVER

Truly, I am to thank you for my degree, if I am.

CRABTREE

Only a friend of Sir Peter's, then, I presume. But, sir, you must have heard of his accident?

SIR OLIVER

Not a word!

CRABTREE

Not of his being dangerously wounded?

SIR OLIVER

The devil he is!

SIR BENJAMIN

Run through the body——

CRABTREE

Shot in the breast——

SIR BENJAMIN

By one Mr. Surface——

CRABTREE

Ay, the younger.

SIR OLIVER

Hey! what the plague! you seem to differ strangely in your accounts: however, you agree that Sir Peter is dangerously wounded.

SIR BENJAMIN

Oh, yes, we agree in that.

CRABTREE

Yes, yes, I believe there can be no doubt in that.

SIR OLIVER

Then, upon my word, for a person in that situation, he is the most imprudent man alive; for here he comes, walking as if nothing at all was the matter.

Enter SIR PETER TEAZLE

Odds heart, Sir Peter! you are come in good time, I promise you; for we had just given you over!

SIR BENJAMIN
[*Aside to* CRABTREE.] Egad, uncle, this is the most sudden recovery!

SIR OLIVER
Why, man! what do you do out of bed with a small-sword through your body, and a bullet lodged in your thorax?

SIR PETER
A small-sword and a bullet?

SIR OLIVER
Ay; these gentlemen would have killed you without law or physic, and wanted to dub me a doctor, to make me an accomplice.

SIR PETER
Why, what is all this?

SIR BENJAMIN
We rejoice, Sir Peter, that the story of the duel is not true, and are sincerely sorry for your other misfortune.

SIR PETER
So, so; all over the town already. [*Aside.*

CRABTREE
Though, Sir Peter, you were certainly vastly to blame to marry at your years.

SIR PETER
Sir, what business is that of yours?

MRS. CANDOUR

Though, indeed, as Sir Peter made so good a husband, he's very much to be pitied.

SIR PETER

Plague on your pity, ma'am! I desire none of it.

SIR BENJAMIN

However, Sir Peter, you must not mind the laughing and jests you will meet with on the occasion.

SIR PETER

Sir, sir! I desire to be master in my own house.

CRABTREE

'Tis no uncommon case, that's one comfort.

SIR PETER

I insist on being left to myself: without ceremony, I insist on your leaving my house directly!

MRS. CANDOUR

Well, well, we are going; and depend on't, we'll make the best report of it we can. [*Exit.*

SIR PETER

Leave my house!

CRABTREE

And tell how hardly you've been treated. [*Exit.*

SIR PETER

Leave my house!

SIR BENJAMIN

And how patiently you bear it. [*Exit.*

SIR PETER

Fiends! vipers! furies! Oh! that their own venom would choke them!

SIR OLIVER

They are very provoking indeed, Sir Peter.

Enter ROWLEY

ROWLEY

I heard high words: what has ruffled you, sir?

SIR PETER

Psha! what signifies asking? Do I ever pass a day without my vexations?

ROWLEY

Well, I'm not inquisitive.

SIR OLIVER

Well, Sir Peter, I have seen both my nephews in the manner we proposed.

SIR PETER

A precious couple they are!

ROWLEY

Yes, and Sir Oliver is convinced that your judgment was right, Sir Peter.

SIR OLIVER

Yes, I find Joseph is indeed the man, after all.

ROWLEY

Ay, as Sir Peter says, he is a man of sentiment.

SIR OLIVER

And acts up to the sentiments he professes.

ROWLEY

It certainly is edification to hear him talk.

SIR OLIVER

Oh, he's a model for the young men of the age! But how's this, Sir Peter? you don't join us in your friend Joseph's praise, as I expected.

SNAKE

SIR PETER

Sir Oliver, we live in a damned wicked world, and the fewer we praise the better.

ROWLEY

What! do you say so, Sir Peter, who were never mistaken in your life?

SIR PETER

Psha! plague on you both! I see by your sneering you have heard the whole affair. I shall go mad among you!

ROWLEY

Then, to fret you no longer, Sir Peter, we are indeed acquainted with it all. I met Lady Teazle coming from Mr. Surface's so humbled, that she deigned to request me to be her advocate with you.

SIR PETER

And does Sir Oliver know all this?

SIR OLIVER

Every circumstance.

SIR PETER

What, of the closet and the screen, hey?

SIR OLIVER

Yes, yes, and the little French milliner. Oh, I have been vastly diverted with the story! ha! ha! ha!

SIR PETER

'Twas very pleasant.

SIR OLIVER

I never laughed more in my life, I assure you: ha! ha! ha!

SIR PETER

Oh, vastly diverting! ha! ha! ha!

ROWLEY

To be sure, Joseph with his sentiments! ha! ha! ha!

SIR PETER

Yes, his sentiments! ha! ha! ha! Hypocritical villain!

SIR OLIVER

Ay, and that rogue Charles to pull Sir Peter out of the closet: ha! ha! ha!

SIR PETER

Ha! ha! 'twas devilish entertaining, to be sure!

SIR OLIVER

Ha! ha! ha! Egad, Sir Peter, I should like to have seen your face when the screen was thrown down: ha! ha!

SIR PETER

Yes, my face when the screen was thrown down: ha! ha! ha! Oh, I must never show my head again!

SIR OLIVER

But come, come, it isn't fair to laugh at you neither, my old friend: though, upon my soul, I can't help it.

SIR PETER

Oh, pray don't restrain your mirth on my account: it does not hurt me at all! I laugh at the whole affair myself. Yes, yes, I think being a standing jest for all one's acquaintance a very happy situation. Oh, yes, and then of a morning to read the paragraphs about Mr. S——, Lady T——, and Sir P——, will be so entertaining!

ROWLEY

Without affectation, Sir Peter, you may despise the ridicule of fools. But I see Lady Teazle going towards the next room; I am sure you must desire a reconciliation as earnestly as she does.

SIR OLIVER

Perhaps my being here prevents her coming to you. Well, I'll leave honest Rowley to mediate between you; but he must bring you all presently to Mr. Surface's, where I am now returning, if not to reclaim a libertine, at least to expose hypocrisy.

SIR PETER

Ah, I'll be present at your discovering yourself there with all my heart; though 'tis a vile unlucky place for discoveries.

ROWLEY

We'll follow.   [*Exit* SIR OLIVER SURFACE.

SIR PETER

She is not coming here, you see, Rowley.

ROWLEY

No, but she has left the door of that room open, you perceive. See, she is in tears.

SIR PETER

Certainly a little mortification appears very becoming in a wife. Don't you think it will do her good to let her pine a little?

ROWLEY

Oh, this is ungenerous in you!

SIR PETER

Well, I know not what to think. You remember the letter I found of hers evidently intended for Charles!

ROWLEY

A mere forgery, Sir Peter! laid in your way on purpose. This is one of the points which I intend Snake shall give you conviction of.

SIR PETER

I wish I were once satisfied of that. She looks this way. What a remarkably elegant turn of the head she has. Rowley, I'll go to her.

ROWLEY

Certainly.

SIR PETER

Though, when it is known that we are reconciled, people will laugh at me ten times more.

ROWLEY

Let them laugh, and retort their malice only by showing them you are happy in spite of it.

SIR PETER

I'faith, so I will! and, if I'm not mistaken, we may yet be the happiest couple in the country.

ROWLEY

Nay, Sir Peter, he who once lays aside suspicion——

SIR PETER

Hold, Master Rowley! if you have any regard for me, never let me hear you utter anything like a sentiment: I have had enough of them to serve me the rest of my life. 　　　　　　　　　　　　　　　　*[Exeunt.*

SCENE THREE

The Library in JOSEPH SURFACE'S *House*

Enter JOSEPH SURFACE *and* LADY SNEERWELL

LADY SNEERWELL

Impossible! Will not Sir Peter immediately be reconciled to Charles, and of course no longer oppose his union with Maria? The thought is distraction to me.

JOSEPH SURFACE

Can passion furnish a remedy?

LADY SNEERWELL

No, nor cunning either. Oh, I was a fool, an idiot, to league with such a blunderer!

JOSEPH SURFACE

Surely, Lady Sneerwell, I am the greatest sufferer; yet you see I bear the accident with calmness.

LADY SNEERWELL

Because the disappointment doesn't reach your heart; your interest only attached you to Maria. Had you felt for her what I have for that ungrateful libertine, neither your temper nor hypocrisy could prevent your showing the sharpness of your vexation.

JOSEPH SURFACE

But why should your reproaches fall on me for this disappointment?

LADY SNEERWELL

Are you not the cause of it? Had you not a sufficient field for your roguery in imposing upon Sir Peter, and supplanting your brother, but you must endeavour to seduce his wife? I hate such an avarice of crimes; 'tis an unfair monopoly, and never prospers.

317

JOSEPH SURFACE

Well, I admit I have been to blame. I confess I deviated from the direct road of wrong, but I don't think we're so totally defeated either.

LADY SNEERWELL

No!

JOSEPH SURFACE

You tell me you have made a trial of Snake since we met, and that you still believe him faithful to us?

LADY SNEERWELL

I do believe so.

JOSEPH SURFACE

And that he has undertaken, should it be necessary, to swear and prove, that Charles is at this time contracted by vows and honour to your ladyship, which some of his former letters to you will serve to support?

LADY SNEERWELL

This, indeed, might have assisted.

JOSEPH SURFACE

Come, come; it is not too late yet.—[*Knocking at the door.*] But hark! this is probably my uncle, Sir Oliver: retire to that room; we'll consult further when he's gone.

LADY SNEERWELL

Well, but if he should find you out too.

JOSEPH SURFACE

Oh, I have no fear of that. Sir Peter will hold his tongue for his own credit's sake—and you may depend on it I shall soon discover Sir Oliver's weak side!

LADY SNEERWELL

I have no diffidence of your abilities! only be constant to one roguery at a time.

JOSEPH SURFACE

I will, I will!—[*Exit* LADY SNEERWELL.] So! 'tis confounded hard, after such bad fortune, to be baited by one's confederate in evil. Well, at all events, my character is so much better than Charles's, that I certainly—hey!—what—this is not Sir Oliver, but old Stanley again. Plague on't that he should return to tease me just now! I shall have Sir Oliver come and find him here—and——

Enter SIR OLIVER SURFACE

Gad's life, Mr. Stanley, why have you come back to plague me at this time? You must not stay now, upon my word.

SIR OLIVER

Sir, I hear your uncle Oliver is expected here, and though he has been so penurious to you, I'll try what he'll do for me.

JOSEPH SURFACE

Sir, 'tis impossible for you to stay now, so I must beg ——Come any other time, and I promise you, you shall be assisted.

SIR OLIVER

No: Sir Oliver and I must be acquainted.

JOSEPH SURFACE

Zounds, sir! then I insist on your quitting the room directly.

SIR OLIVER
Nay, sir——

JOSEPH SURFACE
Sir, I insist on't!—Here, William! show this gentle-man out. Since you compel me, sir, not one moment —this is such insolence.   [*Going to push him out.*

Enter CHARLES SURFACE

CHARLES SURFACE
Heyday! what's the matter now? What the devil have you got hold of my little broker here? Zounds, brother, don't hurt little Premium. What's the matter, my little fellow?

JOSEPH SURFACE
So! he has been with you, too, has he?

CHARLES SURFACE
To be sure he has. Why, he's as honest a little—— But sure, Joseph, you have not been borrowing money too, have you?

JOSEPH SURFACE
Borrowing! no! But, brother, you know we expect Sir Oliver here every——

CHARLES SURFACE
O Gad, that's true! Noll mustn't find the little broker here, to be sure.

JOSEPH SURFACE
Yet, Mr. Stanley insists——

CHARLES SURFACE
Stanley! why his name's Premium.

JOSEPH SURFACE
No, sir, Stanley.

CHARLES SURFACE
No, no, Premium.

JOSEPH SURFACE
Well, no matter which—but——

CHARLES SURFACE
Ay, ay, Stanley or Premium, 'tis the same thing, as you say; for I suppose he goes by half a hundred names, besides A. B. at the coffee-house. [*Knocking.*

JOSEPH SURFACE
'Sdeath! here's Sir Oliver at the door. Now I beg, Mr. Stanley——

CHARLES SURFACE
Ay, ay, and I beg, Mr. Premium——

SIR OLIVER
Gentlemen——

JOSEPH SURFACE
Sir, by heaven you shall go!

CHARLES SURFACE
Ay, out with him, certainly.

SIR OLIVER
This violence——

JOSEPH SURFACE
Sir, 'tis your own fault.

CHARLES SURFACE
Out with him, to be sure.

[*Both forcing* SIR OLIVER *out.*

Enter SIR PETER *and* LADY TEAZLE, MARIA,
and ROWLEY

SIR PETER

My old friend, Sir Oliver—hey! What in the name of wonder!—here are dutiful nephews—assault their uncle at his first visit!

LADY TEAZLE

Indeed, Sir Oliver, 'twas well we came in to rescue you.

ROWLEY

Truly it was; for I perceive, Sir Oliver, the character of old Stanley was no protection to you.

SIR OLIVER

Nor of Premium either: the necessities of the former could not extort a shilling from that benevolent gentleman; and with the other I stood a chance of faring worse than my ancestors, and being knocked down without being bid for.

JOSEPH SURFACE
Charles!

CHARLES SURFACE
Joseph!

JOSEPH SURFACE
'Tis now complete!

CHARLES SURFACE
Very.

SIR OLIVER
Sir Peter, my friend, and Rowley too—look on that elder nephew of mine. You know what he has already received from my bounty; and you also know how

gladly I would have regarded half my fortune as held in trust for him? judge, then, my disappointment in discovering him to be destitute of truth, charity, and gratitude!

SIR PETER

Sir Oliver, I should be more surprised at this declaration, if I had not myself found him to be mean, treacherous, and hypocritical.

LADY TEAZLE

And if the gentleman pleads not guilty to these, pray let him call me to his character.

SIR PETER

Then, I believe, we need add no more: if he knows himself, he will consider it as the most perfect punishment that he is known to the world.

CHARLES SURFACE

If they talk this way to Honesty, what will they say to me, by-and-by?   [*Aside.*

[SIR PETER, LADY TEAZLE, *and* MARIA *retire.*

SIR OLIVER

As for that prodigal, his brother, there——

CHARLES SURFACE

Ay, now comes my turn: the damned family pictures will ruin me!   [*Aside.*

JOSEPH SURFACE

Sir Oliver—uncle, will you honour me with a hearing.

CHARLES SURFACE

Now, if Joseph would make one of his long speeches, I might recollect myself a little.   [*Aside.*

SIR OLIVER

I suppose you would undertake to justify yourself?

[*To* JOSEPH SURFACE.

JOSEPH SURFACE

I trust I could.

SIR OLIVER

[*To* CHARLES SURFACE.] Well, sir!—and you could justify yourself too, I suppose?

CHARLES SURFACE

Not that I know of, Sir Oliver.

SIR OLIVER

What!—Little Premium has been let too much into the secret, I suppose?

CHARLES SURFACE

True, sir; but they were family secrets, and should not be mentioned again, you know.

ROWLEY

Come, Sir Oliver, I know you cannot speak of Charles's follies with anger.

SIR OLIVER

Odd's heart, no more I can; nor with gravity either. Sir Peter, do you know the rogue bargained with me for all his ancestors; sold me judges and generals by the foot, and maiden aunts as cheap as broken china.

CHARLES SURFACE

To be sure, Sir Oliver, I did make a little free with the family canvas, that's the truth on't. My ancestors may rise in judgment against me, there's no denying it; but believe me sincere when I tell you—and upon my soul I would not say so if I was not—that if I do not appear mortified at the exposure of my follies, it is because I feel at this moment the warmest satisfaction at seeing you, my liberal benefactor.

SIR OLIVER

Charles, I believe you. Give me your hand again: the ill-looking little fellow over the settee has made your peace.

CHARLES SURFACE

Then, sir, my gratitude to the original is still increased.

LADY TEAZLE

[*Advancing.*] Yet, I believe, Sir Oliver, here is one whom Charles is still more anxious to be reconciled to.   [*Pointing to* MARIA.

SIR OLIVER

Oh, I have heard of his attachment there; and, with the young lady's pardon, if I construe right—that blush——

SIR PETER

Well, child, speak your sentiments.

MARIA

Sir, I have little to say, but that I shall rejoice to hear that he is happy; for me, whatever claim I had to his attention, I willingly resign to one who has a better title.

CHARLES SURFACE

How, Maria!

SIR PETER

Heyday! what's the mystery now? While he appeared an incorrigible rake, you would give your hand to no one else; and now that he is likely to reform I'll warrant you won't have him.

MARIA
His own heart and Lady Sneerwell know the cause.

CHARLES SURFACE
Lady Sneerwell!

JOSEPH SURFACE
Brother, it is with great concern I am obliged to speak on this point, but my regard to justice compels me, and Lady Sneerwell's injuries can no longer be concealed.   [*Opens the door.*

Enter LADY SNEERWELL

SIR PETER
So! another French milliner! Egad, he has one in every room in the house, I suppose!

LADY SNEERWELL
Ungrateful Charles! Well may you be surprised, and feel for the indelicate situation your perfidy has forced me into.

CHARLES SURFACE
Pray, uncle, is this another plot of yours? For, as I have life, I don't understand it.

JOSEPH SURFACE
I believe, sir, there is but the evidence of one person more necessary to make it extremely clear.

SIR PETER
And that person, I imagine, is Mr. Snake.—Rowley, you were perfectly right to bring him with us, and pray let him appear.

ROWLEY

Walk in, Mr. Snake.

Enter SNAKE

I thought his testimony might be wanted; however, it happens unluckily, that he comes to confront Lady Sneerwell, not to support her.

LADY SNEERWELL

A villain! Treacherous to me at last! Speak, fellow, have you too conspired against me?

SNAKE

I beg your ladyship ten thousand pardons: you paid me extremely liberally for the lie in question; but I unfortunately have been offered double to speak the truth.

LADY SNEERWELL

The torments of shame and disappointment on you all! [*Going.*

LADY TEAZLE

Hold, Lady Sneerwell—before you go, let me thank you for the trouble you and that gentleman have taken, in writing letters from me to Charles, and answering them yourself; and let me also request you to make my respects to the scandalous college, of which you are president, and inform them, that Lady Teazle, licentiate, begs leave to return the diploma they granted her, as she leaves off practice, and kills characters no longer.

LADY SNEERWELL

You too, madam!—provoking—insolent! May your husband live these fifty years! [*Exit.*

SIR PETER
Oons! what a fury!

LADY TEAZLE
A malicious creature, indeed!

SIR PETER
What! not for her last wish?

LADY TEAZLE
Oh, no!

SIR OLIVER
Well, sir, and what have you to say now?

JOSEPH SURFACE
Sir, I am so confounded, to find that Lady Sneerwell could be guilty of suborning Mr. Snake in this manner, to impose on us all, that I know not what to say: however, lest her revengeful spirit should prompt her to injure my brother, I had certainly better follow her directly.   [*Exit.*

SIR PETER
Moral to the last drop!

SIR OLIVER
Ay, and marry her, Joseph, if you can. Oil and vinegar!—egad you'll do very well together.

ROWLEY
I believe we have no more occasion for Mr. Snake at present?

SNAKE
Before I go, I beg pardon once for all, for whatever uneasiness I have been the humble instrument of causing to the parties present.

328

SIR PETER

Well, well, you have made atonement by a good deed at last.

SNAKE

But I must request of the company, that it shall never be known.

SIR PETER

Hey! what the plague! are you ashamed of having done a right thing once in your life?

SNAKE

Ah, sir, consider—I live by the badness of my character; and, if it were once known that I had been betrayed into an honest action, I should lose every friend I have in the world.

SIR OLIVER

Well, well—we'll not traduce you by saying anything in your praise, never fear.   [*Exit* SNAKE.

SIR PETER

There's a precious rogue!

LADY TEAZLE

See, Sir Oliver, there needs no persuasion now to reconcile your nephew and Maria.

SIR OLIVER

Ay, ay, that's as it should be, and, egad, we'll have the wedding to-morrow morning.

CHARLES SURFACE

Thank you, dear uncle.

SIR PETER

What, you rogue! don't you ask the girl's consent first?

CHARLES SURFACE

Oh, I have done that a long time—a minute ago—and she has looked yes.

MARIA

For shame, Charles!—I protest, Sir Peter, there has not been a word——

SIR OLIVER

Well, then, the fewer the better: may your love for each other never know abatement.

SIR PETER

And may you live as happily together as Lady Teazle and I intend to do!

CHARLES SURFACE

Rowley, my old friend, I am sure you congratulate me; and I suspect that I owe you much.

SIR OLIVER

You do, indeed, Charles.

ROWLEY

If my efforts to serve you had not succeeded you would have been in my debt for the attempt—but deserve to be happy—and you over-repay me.

SIR PETER

Ay, honest Rowley always said you would reform.

CHARLES SURFACE

Why as to reforming, Sir Peter, I'll make no promises,
and that I take to be a proof that I intend to set about
it. But here shall be my monitor—my gentle guide.—
Ah! can I leave the virtuous path those eyes illumine?

Though thou, dear maid, shouldst wave thy beauty's
    sway,
Thou still must rule, because I will obey:
An humble fugitive from Folly view,
No sanctuary near but Love and you: [*To the audience.*
You can, indeed, each anxious fear remove,
For even Scandal dies, if you approve. [*Exeunt omnes.*

EPILOGUE

By Mr. Colman

SPOKEN BY LADY TEAZLE

I, who was late so volatile and gay,
Like a trade-wind must now blow all one way,
Bend all my cares, my studies, and my vows,
To one dull rusty weathercock—my spouse!
So wills our virtuous bard—the motley Bayes
Of crying epilogues and laughing plays!
Old bachelors, who marry smart young wives,
Learn from our play to regulate your lives:
Each bring his dear to town, all faults upon her—
London will prove the very source of honour.
Plunged fairly in, like a cold bath it serves,
When principles relax, to brace the nerves:
Such is my case; and yet I must deplore
That the gay dream of dissipation's o'er.
And say, ye fair! was ever lively wife,
Born with a genius for the highest life,
Like me untimely blasted in her bloom,
Like me condemn'd to such a dismal doom?
Save money—when I just knew how to waste it!
Leave London—just as I began to taste it!
Must I then watch the early crowing cock,
The melancholy ticking of a clock;
In a lone rustic hall for ever pounded,

With dogs, cats, rats, and squalling brats surrounded?
With humble curate can I now retire,
(While good Sir Peter boozes with the squire,)
And at backgammon mortify my soul,
That pants for loo, or flutters at a vole.
Seven's the main! Dear sound that must expire,
Lost at hot cockles round a Christmas fire;
The transient hour of fashion too soon spent,
Farewell the tranquil mind, farewell content!
Farewell the plumèd head, the cushion'd tête,
That takes the cushion from its proper seat!
That spirit-stirring drum!—card drums I mean,
Spadille—odd trick—pam—basto—king and queen!
And you, ye knockers, that, with brazen throat,
The welcome visitors' approach denote;
Farewell all quality of high renown,
Pride, pomp, and circumstance of glorious town!
Farewell! your revels I partake no more,
And Lady Teazle's occupation's o'er!
All this I told our bard; he smiled, and said 'twas clear,
I ought to play deep tragedy next year.
Meanwhile he drew wise morals from his play,
And in these solemn periods stalk'd away:—
'Bless'd were the fair like you; her faults who stopp'd,
And closed her follies when the curtain dropp'd!
No more in vice or error to engage,
Or play the fool at large on life's great stage.'